D1565935

CAUSE and CIRCUMSTANCE

CAUSE and CIRCUMSTANCE

Aircraft Accidents and How to Avoid Them

ARCHIE TRAMMELL

Ziff-Davis Publishing Company/New York

Manufactured in the United States of America
First Printing 1980.
Library of Congress Catalog Number 79-66679
ISBN 0-87165-042-8
Ziff-Davis Publishing Company
One Park Avenue
New York, New York 10016

DEDICATION

This book is dedicated to those airmen who were
involved in the accidents cited. By examining their
misfortunes, the rest of us may avoid a similar fate.

CONTENTS

FOREWORD

The greatest possible privilege in aviation journalism is the opportunity to write on aviation safety. You have a good feeling each night, knowing that something you wrote during the day will certainly save a life and may even prevent a major disaster.

For six years as editor of *Business and Commercial Aviation* Magazine, I enjoyed that privilege. Many of the safety articles I wrote appeared as feature stories or in the monthly editorial, but I also—quite selfishly, I admit—reserved the "Cause and Circumstance" column for my exclusive byline. I drew great satisfaction from each of the 62 "C and C" columns I wrote from July 1972 through May 1978. Now I have a double privilege in being given the opportunity to edit 48 of those columns for this book. The originals were written for *Business and Commercial Aviation* Magazine's audience of professional and semi-professional pilots of higher performance piston aircraft and corporate turboprops and jets. Yet I hope that all pilots of all classes of equipment will become safer airmen as a result of reading the edited versions which appear in the following pages. For the sake of clarity, I have indicated the month and year of each article's appearance in *B/CA*.

So, as you re-experience six years of the "Cause and Circumstance" column, please forgive my frequent references to business flying and my occasional references to periods in aviation that have passed.

Hindsight is 20/20 and I have become a safer pilot from looking

FOREWORD

back and writing about aviation accidents of the recent past. Please read about the mistakes of others in the same spirit—and keep your nose down throughout your flying career.

ARCHIE TRAMMELL
Fort Lauderdale, Florida
June 1979

CAUSE and CIRCUMSTANCE

THE CLASSICS 1

Perhaps no accident should be dignified
with the term "classic," but three in the
"Cause and Circumstance" series are so
archetypal, they can be called nothing less.

The Boston Crash: A Classic–Approach Accident (July 1974)

One is reluctant to glorify a crash in which 89 people died by
referring to it as "classic," but this one certainly was. For years
to come, whether they're looking for poor human factors in equipment design, ATC system failures, or pilot error as the cause,
researchers and writers will be referring to the July 1973 crash
of a DC–9 at Boston as the "textbook" accident. Let's look at it
from all three of those angles, one or more of which is a basic
cause in every approach mishap.

Poor human factors. The DC-9, operating as Delta Flight 723,
departed Manchester, New Hampshire at 1050 hours for an 18-
minute flight to Boston's Logan Airport. The plane had been held
on the ground 53 minutes after leaving the gate at Manchester
due to Boston weather. It was cleared to the Lawrence, Massachu-
setts VOR, then vectored for a Runway 4 Right ILS approach to
Logan. After an erratic approach in near zero/zero visibility, it
crashed into a seawall 3000 feet short of the displaced Runway 4R
threshold, 165 feet to the right of centerline and approximately

1

nine feet below the level of the runway. The wreckage bounded over the seawall and scattered along the displaced threshold.

Among the things the National Transportation Safety Board discovered in its investigation was that the flight director mode–selector installed in the aircraft could easily be mismanaged. The NTSB stopped short of saying the selector had a trap built into it, but we will say it.

It was a rotary–type switch, beginning with a standby position and then going clockwise through backcourse, "flight instruments" (basic attitude), VOR/LOC, approach, and go–around modes. The flight director system had no mode–annunciator other than the selector itself.

Normally, in an approach it would be set to the VOR/LOC position. When operating in that mode, glideslope capture is automatic, but *only* if the glideslope is approached from *below*. Flight 723, however, was vectored onto the ILS from *above* the glideslope.

In that situation, the horizontal command bar is biased out of sight until the switch is rotated to the next clockwise position (APP), which causes the pitch bar to appear and give glideslope commands. If the switch is slightly over–rotated through the APP mode—as can easily happen when the crew is rushed—the go-around mode is selected. In the go-around mode, the vertical bar stays in sight, as though still giving localizer information, but it actually commands wings level only, and the horizontal bar comes into view showing a fly–up command, which can cause confusion if raw data is showing an above–glideslope condition.

In fact, the crew *was* rushed; the selector in the crashed DC–9 *was* found in the go–around position; the flight data recorder trace shows that indeed the aircraft *was* above glideslope until 51 seconds before impact. Furthermore, the crew was obviously experiencing doubts about the flight director indications. One min-

2

ute before impact the copilot, who was flying the aircraft, re-marked, "This #@! command bar shows (unintelligible word)."

The captain replied, "Yeah, that doesn't show much."

Thirty-five seconds later, only 25 seconds prior to impact, the captain said, "You better go to raw data. I don't trust that thing."

As a result of those findings, the NTSB recommended that all flight directors incorporate an annunciator that clearly indicates the mode on which the system is operating, regardless of which mode has been selected.

Systems failures. At this point one should logically ask: Why was the crew rushed? And why were they shooting an approach in zero-zero conditions? The answer: Because both the ATC and the weather reporting *systems broke down.*

The ATC broke down when the approach controller fell behind in issuing instructions to the crew of Flight 723. He issued vital instructions late or not at all. Just after the controller had descended Flight 723 to 3000 feet and had given the initial vector for the ILS, his attention was drawn away by a potential conflict between two other aircraft. As a result of the crew's not being given a second vector, the ILS was intercepted at an angle of 45 degrees and the crew overshot the inbound turn. They were not told where they would intercept the ILS relative to the outer marker and so turned inbound while still steaming along at better than 220 knots. They were not cleared for the approach until they questioned the controller about it, just 35 seconds before crossing the outer marker, at which time they were already one dot high on the glideslope as well as 55 knots fast.

It's doubtful if anyone could have shot a smooth approach after getting sandbagged like that. The NTSB said as much in the accident report: " . . . through experience and exposure to instrument approaches during instrument meteorological conditions, pilots generally learn to pace their ac⁺ivities while flying such an approach. The faster–than–normal airspeed of Flight 723 during the initial and final phases of its approach required the crew to act more quickly than usual."

This brings up an interesting point: When a pilot gets behind his airplane during an approach, he's expected to break off and try again. Why isn't there a similar requirement for controllers? They have missed approaches, too. And they have them often. I experience about one controller–missed–approach for every 30 approaches in actual IFR conditions.

This is no reflection on the ATC controller as a professional. He's only human. Pilots blow about one in 30 approaches themselves. The point is that airplanes can get bent just as violently when controllers try to save a botched approach as they can when pilots try to patch one up.

Therefore, since pilots are supposed to swallow their pride, admit a mistake and request another approach when necessary, it's far more incumbent on controllers to do so. This course of action is implied in the *Air Traffic Control Handbook,* but I have yet to hear a controller say, "Sorry, I made an error so I'm going to vector you around for another try," which is precisely what the controller of Flight 723 should have done when the crew called just 1.74 nm outside the marker at an assigned altitude 1000 feet *above* the crossing altitude and *asked* for an approach clearance.

The crew was also let down by the weather system. When they began the approach, they were told the weather was "partial obscuration, estimated 400 overcast, mile and a half and fog." Only 20 seconds before impact, the crew was told, "Cleared to land 4R. Traffic is clearing at the end. The RVR shows more than 6000. A fog bank is moving in. It's pretty heavy across the approach end."

As it happens, the RVR (Runway Visual Range) was actually below minimums at that instant. It has never been made clear to either controllers or pilots, but RVR values are subject to massive errors. They do not measure actual runway visual range; they measure visual range off to the side of the runway. Also, an RVR updates only once each 51.1 seconds. A lot can happen to weather conditions in less than a minute. At BOS that day a fog bank rolled in, dropping the RVR to between 1600 and 2000 feet within seconds. It was several minutes before the controllers realized that the airport was below minimums. The crash of Flight 723 was not seen from the tower cab because visibility was so poor. In fact, two flights following 723 shot missed approaches because of the weather before it was discovered that the DC-9 was scattered along the active runway.

Pilot error. In spite of the overwhelming evidence that both the equipment onboard and the ATC and weather systems had let the crew down, the NTSB concluded that the accident was the result of *pilot error:* "The NTSB determines that the probable cause of the accident was the failure of the flight crew to monitor altitude and to recognize passage of the aircraft through the approach decision height . . ."

Some help. The purpose of an accident investigation should be to prevent future similar accidents. Telling pilots not to get too low—as the NTSB did in this case—isn't going to accomplish that. Ever since Orville and Wilbur first busted a landing skid on the sands of Kitty Hawk, we've all known that flying into the ground is a messy way to terminate a flight. It's undoubtedly accurate to say we all try to avoid such a termination.

Although on Friday night when we gather around the bar we may not talk like it, pilots are ordinary mortals. Put enough pressure on any of us and we'll do something stupid—like forget to monitor altitude. After a couple of million years of waiting, by now it should be obvious that the Almighty is not going to create a perfect cadre of men and women for occupations that are unforgiving of human frailty.

Most serious pilots are probably at least 90 percent as safe as it's possible to become in the aeronautical environment without Divine help. We pilots must continue to work toward improvement —through books and articles, studies, seminars, retraining, and occasional regulatory changes. But as in anything else, once you achieve 90 percent perfection, that last 10 percent is extremely difficult to attain. The next significant gains in safety must come from improved human factors and better presentation of vital information.

Consider the human factors involved in the final flight of this DC–9 crew. First, ATC busted the approach. Next, technology let them down with poorly designed equipment. Finally, they were told that visibility was more than a mile and that the aircraft preceding them had landed and was taxiing clear.

This put enormous pressure on them. The first officer was flying and no doubt was putting his trust in the captain; the captain was busy trying to correct the flight director malfunction as well as talking his copilot through the approach so as not to put him down by assuming control. There was an observer in the cockpit (a fellow pilot returning to duty after a long illness), which would have made a missed approach doubly embarrassing. Most important, because the aircraft in front of them had landed, the crew had every reason to believe they would break out—as they had thousands of times previously—before hitting something.

Placing more gadgets in the cockpit is seldom the total answer to a safety problem, but in the area of approach accidents, gadgetry seems to be dragging the horse behind it. We've invented, developed, legislated and regulated all kinds of en-route safety and convenience devices into cockpits, but the final altitude gadget is still the baro altimeter that Jimmy Doolittle used back in 1929 on the first IFR approach. Radio altimeters should have been an advancement, but this DC–9 had one; the crew discussed setting it to DH and still flew into the ground.

Ironically, the FAA has developed in–house something that may be better. It's a simple recording of a female voice, hooked to a volume control that is governed by raw data from the glide-slope needle's displacement. If one of these had been installed in this DC–9 the lady would have begun telling the crew they were too low just past the middle marker and would have been shouting at them at impact.

Perhaps that device or a similar one developed privately by Sundstrand could have saved this crew. In any event, it seems to us that rather than blame the crew for a natural, predictable human failure, we ought to be taking a harder look at ways to correct human frailties by coming up with a simple, inexpensive device to replace all those expensive ones we now have in the cockpit, put there by regulations, that aren't getting the job done.

Wind Shear at JFK (June 1976)

The NTSB report on the crash of an Eastern 727 at JFK in June 1975 held no surprises. The Board's exhaustive investigation disclosed that Flight 66 probably had encountered a severe wind shear at about 500 feet msl while conducting an ILS to Runway 22L. The initial downdraft was about 16 feet per second (960 fpm) coupled with a 15–knot increase in the headwind component. The downdraft then increased to 21 feet per second (1260 fpm) coupled with a 15–knot *decrease* in the headwind component. The shear was caused by a thunderstorm that was straddling the ILS course. The NTSB did a better than average job in compiling this report, (No. NTSB–AAR–76–8, available from the National Technical Information Service, Springfield, Virginia 22151) and we recommend that every pilot and flight department manager read it thoroughly.

Two questions about this accident are particularly important. First: Why was the captain shooting an approach through a thunderstorm? Second: Why didn't anyone on the flight deck notice the high sink rate until it was too late?

The answer to the first question is complex. Evidently the captain really didn't want to fly through a thunderstorm, but captains ahead of him were doing it, so he felt he had to give it a try.

Here's a portion of the NTSB's analysis—the parenthesized comments are the captain's:

> The Safety Board sought to determine why the captain of Eastern 66 continued his approach to Runway 22L. The captain had received only one report of adverse conditions—the report from Eastern 902. This report apparently disturbed the captain (" . . . this is asinine"), but it also apparently was quickly rationalized to some degree ("I wonder if they're covering for themselves"). Had the captain known that two flights had reported adverse conditions, rationalization probably would have been more difficult. However, had he decided to make his approach to a different runway, he probably would have been delayed up to an additional 30 minutes because simultaneous instrument approach operations could not be conducted to two different runways. A 30–minute delay would have reduced substantially his fuel reserve of about one hour. Considering the thunderstorm activity affecting the New York City area, including his alternate airport, La Guardia, his fuel reserve would have been minimal.
>
> It is uncertain when the captain of Eastern 66 made his final decision to continue the approach. He apparently had not made a final determination when the flight was five miles from the OM and was cleared for the approach because he told the final vector controller, " . . . we'll let you know about conditions." Also, about a minute later, he explained to the first officer, "I have the radar on standby in case I need it . . . . ", which suggests he was thinking about the possibility of either making the approach or having to abandon it. However, because pilots commonly rely on the degree of success achieved

by pilots of preceding flights when they are confronted with common hazards, it is likely that he continued the approach pending receipt of information on the progress of the two flights which were immediately ahead of him. By the time the second of these two flights had landed without reported difficulty, the captain of Eastern 66 was apparently committed to the approach, which discloses the hazards of reliance on the success of pilots of preceding flights when dynamic and severe weather conditions exist.

This situation is something for us all to think about carefully. No captain should allow the captain of another aircraft to make his decisions for him. The old rule—if you have doubts, don't try it—needs to be written with Y-O-U, in capitals.

The question of why the crew didn't notice the high sink rate is also answered by the NTSB. To set the stage, the first officer was flying and the captain was monitoring. Reported visibility was two miles, but a heavy rain shower at the end of the runway reduced actual visibility to less than a mile.

In that setting, here's what happened, as reported by the NTSB:

At 1604:38.3, N8845E was nearly centered on the glide-slope when the flight engineer called, "500 feet." The airspeed was oscillating between 140 and 148 knots. The sound of heavy rain could be heard as the aircraft descended below 500 feet, and the windshield wipers were switched to high speed.

At 1604:40.5, the captain said, "Stay on the gauges." The first officer responded, "Oh, yes. I'm right with it." At 1604:-48.0, the flight engineer said, "Three greens, 30 degrees, final checklist," and the captain responded, "Right."

At 1604:52.6, the captain said, "I have approach lights," and the first officer said, "Okay." At 1604:54.7, the captain again said, "Stay on the gauges," and the first officer replied, "I'm with it." N8845E then was passing through 400 feet, and

9

its rate of descent increased from an average of about 675 feet per minute (fpm) to 1500 fpm. The aircraft rapidly began to deviate below the glideslope, and four seconds later, the airspeed decreased from 138 knots to 123 knots in 2.5 seconds.

N8845E continued to deviate further below the glideslope, and at 1605:06.2, when the aircraft was at 150 feet, the captain said, "Runway lights in sight." Less than a second later, the first officer said, "I got it." The captain replied, "Got it?" and a second later, at 1605:10.2, an unintelligible exclamation was recorded, and the first officer commanded, "Takeoff thrust." The sound of impact was recorded at 1605:11.4

Anyone who has ever shot a tight approach as part of a two–person crew knows what happened. Here it is, as analyzed by the Board:

> Throughout the time period, the captain probably was looking outside, because about six seconds before the rate of descent began to increase he called, "I have approach lights" and about seven seconds after the rate began to increase he called, "Runway in sight." At the time of the latter call, the airplane was descending rapidly through 150 feet and was about 80 feet below the glideslope—twice the distance that would have produced a full–scale "fly–up" indication on the related flight instruments if the glideslope signal was reliable. The Safety Board believes that the first officer's immediate response, "I got it," to the captain's identification of the runway indicates that the first officer had probably been looking outside or was alternating his scan between the flight instruments and the approach lights.

How many times must it be written: Stay on the instruments until the landing is assured. Twice in a period of 20 seconds, the captain told his first officer, "Stay on the gauges." But evidently the pilot at the controls came off the instruments when the aircraft was still 100 or 200 feet above decision height.

Besides reminding us that subordinates should heed the captain if the job is going to be done right, this accident demonstrates that a procedure which has the head–down man staying head down throughout a tight approach, with the head–up man taking over for touchdown, is the only way to fly a two–pilot approach. Think about that carefully.

The Short Carefree Life of a Scudrunner (August 1974)

In September 1973, a Texas International Airlines Convair 600 flew into a mountain in western Arkansas at night while penetrating a line of thunderstorms. The following April, less than seven months after the accident, in which the three crew and eight passengers perished, the NTSB issued its report on the probable cause.

A period of only six months from the crash of an air carrier to completion of the investigation may be an NTSB record. The reason for the speed is simple: All the investigators had to do was listen to the cockpit voice recorder and the cause of the crash was dramatically narrated by the crew itself.

Let's first set the scene: TI Flight 655 was on a round–robin flight, Dallas–Memphis–Dallas, with intermediate stops. At 1953, on the return leg, the flight landed at El Dorado, in western Arkansas, for a brief stop before proceeding on to Texarkana, 60 nm west northwest of El Dorado on the Arkansas/-Texas border. Inbound to El Dorado the crew reported "painting a solid line (of thunderstorms) about 50 miles west of El Dorado."

After landing at El Dorado, the crew discussed the weather with Flight Service Station personnel and two other westbound pilots. The two other pilots in time deviated south successfully through the squall line in light precip and little turbulence. However, Flight 655 departed (at 2015) without an IFR flight plan and proceeded northwest VFR along the route depicted in the illustration.

After departure the crew made no attempt to contact any ground facility. The first officer was flying the aircraft. Here, excerpted from the cockpit voice recorder installed in the TI Convair, is what the crew discussed. Asterisks indicate deleted expletives.

The first conversation begins a couple of minutes after departure. It obviously centers on the line of thunderstorms immediately west of El Dorado in the direction of Texarkana, which they were studying on their airborne radar.

CAPTAIN: That might not be a hole there.

FIRST OFFICER: We'll know shortly. It sorta looks like 24 miles to the end. I don't mind, do you?

CAPTAIN: I don't care, just as long as we don't go through it.

FIRST OFFICER: Looks a little strange through there. Looks like something attenuating through there. It's a shadow.

CAPTAIN: Yeah, looks like a shadow.

FIRST OFFICER: See something?

CAPTAIN: I think it's snow.

FIRST OFFICER: I still think that's a shadow. Wanna go around?

CAPTAIN: Yeah, why not?

(Approximately 12 minutes into the flight.)

FIRST OFFICER: I thought the end of that line was way back down over there, now . . . , keeps growing on us.

CAPTAIN: No, not really.

(Approximately 16 minutes into the flight.)

FIRST OFFICER: It's a real cute li'l old curleycue, ain't it?

CAPTAIN: Yeah, ha, ha. There's not much to that, but we gotta stay away from it 'cause we'll be vee . . . IFR.

FIRST OFFICER: Si. * I can't get this * stupid radar **. You got any idea where we're at?

CAPTAIN: Yeah, two sixteen'll take us right to the VOR.

12

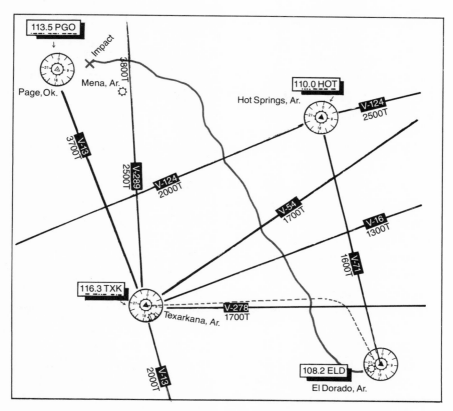

Normal IFR routing El Dorado to Texarkana would be Victor 278, as shown by the dashed line. In attempting to end-run a squall line, this crew flew northwest, as indicated by the solid line at 2000 to 3000 feet —sometimes in cloud. Notice the minimum terrain–clearance altitudes for the various airways.

FIRST OFFICER: Two, ah . . .

CAPTAIN: Two–oh–nine, I got.

FIRST OFFICER: Fifteen.

CAPTAIN: I'm not concerned with that, I could care less. I guess you're right. That . . . that is just extending on and on and on as we go along 'cause it hasn't moved in about three or four miles in the last 30 minutes, it seems like.

FIRST OFFICER: We don't want to get too far up the ****. It gets hilly.

CAPTAIN: Yeah. Stars are shining. Why don't you try 2000?

[The captain was referring to a reduction in the aircraft's altitude to 2000 feet. The flight was never above 3000 feet mean sea level during the entire episode.]

(Approximately 19 minutes into the flight.)

CAPTAIN: If we get up here anywhere near Hot Springs, we get in the * mountains.

FIRST OFFICER: Uh, you reckon there's a ridge line along here somewhere?

FIRST OFFICER (?): Let's go ahead and try for 2500.

CAPTAIN: All right. Fred, you can quit worrying about the mountains 'cause that'll clear everything over there.

FIRST OFFICER: That's why I wanted to go to 2500 feet. That's the Hot Springs highway right here, I think.

CAPTAIN: You 'bout right.

FIRST OFFICER: Texarkan' . . . naw, it ain't either. *, Texarkana's back here.

CAPTAIN: Texarkana's back over here, somewhere.

FIRST OFFICER: Yeah. This ain't no Hot Springs highway.

(Approximately 20 minutes into the flight.)

CAPTAIN: Well, 30 degrees . . . 30 degrees takes you right to Texarkana doesn't it? Hot Springs . . . here we are sittin' on 50.

FIRST OFFICER: Yeah. How we doin' on that ** **? Look how we're gainin' on the ground.

14

CAPTAIN: I don't know, Fred, still we keep getting another one poppin' up every time . . . every time.

FIRST OFFICER: There ain't no lights on the ground over there.

CAPTAIN: Yeah, I see 'em behind us. See stars above us.

(Approximately 23 minutes into the flight.)

FIRST OFFICER: I got some lights on the ground.

CAPTAIN: There's just not many out here.

FIRST OFFICER: Maybe . . . could be somethin' else, coach.

CAPTAIN: Aha, we're gettin' rid of the clouds . . . . We is in the clouds, Fred.

FIRST OFFICER: Are we?

CAPTAIN: Yea . . . No, we're not . . . I can see above us.

(Approximately 24 minutes into the flight.)

FIRST OFFICER: Now, what have we got here?

CAPTAIN: Naw, you're all right, I can see some lights over here.

FIRST OFFICER: I'll tell ya what, coach . . . . That's probably Hot Springs.

CAPTAIN: Yep, could be. Yeah, that might be either it or Arkadelphia.

FIRST OFFICER: Well, I'm getting out of the clouds here Mac, but I'm getting right straight into it.

CAPTAIN: Oh, looks like you're all right.

FIRST OFFICER: Do you see any stars above us? We're going in and outta some scud.

CAPTAIN: Yeah, we've got a little bit here.

FIRST OFFICER: I sure wish I knew where the * we were.

(Approximately 26 minutes into the flight.)

FIRST OFFICER: Paintin' ridges and everything else, boss, and I'm not familiar with the terrain. We're staying in the clouds.

CAPTAIN: Yeah, I'd stay down. You're right in the . . . right in the base of the clouds. I tell you what—we're gonna be able to turn here in a minute.

(Approximately 30 minutes into the flight.)

FIRST OFFICER: I can see the ground now.

CAPTAIN: Keep on truckin', just keep on a–truckin'.

FIRST OFFICER: Well, we must be somewhere in Oklahoma.

CAPTAIN: Doin' all the good in the world.

FIRST OFFICER: Do you have any idea what the frequency of the Paris VOR is?

UNIDENTIFIED: Nope, don't really give a *.

(Approximately 33 minutes into the flight.)

CAPTAIN: Put, uh, about 265 heading 265.

FIRST OFFICER: Heading, 265. I would say we * up.

CAPTAIN: Think so?

UNIDENTIFIED: *(Laughter)*

CAPTAIN: Fred, descend to 2000.

FIRST OFFICER: Two thousand. Coming down . . . Here we are, we're not out of it.

CAPTAIN: Let's truck on . . . . First time I've ever made a mistake in my life.

(Approximately 34 minutes into the flight.)

FIRST OFFICER: I'll be *. Man, I wish I knew where we were so we'd have some idea of the general * terrain around this * place.

CAPTAIN: I know what it is.

FIRST OFFICER: What?

CAPTAIN: That the highest point out here is about 1200 feet. . . . The whole general area—and then we're not even where that is, I don't believe.

UNIDENTIFIED: *(Whistling)*

CAPTAIN: Go ahead and look at it.

UNIDENTIFIED: *(Whistling)*

UNIDENTIFIED: *

UNIDENTIFIED: *(Whistling)*

(Approximately 37 minutes into the flight.)

FIRST OFFICER: Two hundred fifty, we're about to pass over Page VOR. . . . You know where that is?

16

CAPTAIN: Yeah.

FIRST OFFICER: All right.

CAPTAIN: About 180 degrees to Texarkana.

FIRST OFFICER: 'About 152 . . . Minimum en-route altitude is 44 hund . . .'

[The final sound on the cockpit voice recorder is of the impact with a ridge.]

The lessons to be gained from this accident are so clear they need not be stated.

FATIGUE

2

When a pilot is tired, errors in judgment are certain to occur. Add one stroke of ill-fate and suddenly the errors snowball.

The Frobisher Sabreliner Crash (January 1975)

There is an ancient saying in aviation that is so corny most of us are embarrassed to repeat it to our peers. Nevertheless, its sentiment needs to be recalled by all pilots every now and then: The sky, to an even greater extent than the sea, is terribly unforgiving of errors.

That truth shows clearly in the crash of a Sabre 40 which, in February 1974, was flown out of fuel just 65 miles short of Frobisher Bay in northern Canada on a flight from Keflavik, Iceland.

A study of the accident by the Aviation Safety Division of the Canadian Ministry of Transportation (MoT) indicates that the aircraft was sound, and that the crew prepared for and conducted the flight within the bounds of work-a-day professionalism. The accident apparently resulted from a string of hard luck (which even in combination should not have caused such a mishap), plus a single error by the crew that in other circumstances would have been minor.

The aircraft was a Sabreliner Model NA265–40 under Canadian registry, CF–BRL. It had been flown 675.5 hours, and the records and evidence indicate it was properly maintained and capable of the trip. The captain was ATP–rated with 13,500 hours total time —3000 hours of it in business jets and 346 hours in the Sabreliner. He had made 800 Atlantic crossings, *including 20 in this same aircraft.*

The copilot had 8700 hours—1200 in jets and 217 in the Sabreliner. He was commercially rated, but his instrument rating had been allowed to expire on January 1 before the accident. There was no evidence of incapacitation or illness of either crewmember.

Using the brief facts and times given in the report, let's reconstruct the trip. The aircraft was flown to Stuttgart, Germany on or about February 24, presumably by this same crew. After a two-day layover in Stuttgart, on February 27 at 1437 hours Greenwich Mean Time, the aircraft departed Stuttgart for Toronto via Frobisher with its crew and seven passengers.

It is important to consider that time of departure. The Canadian authorities did not, but we feel it has major significance. The local time was 1:37 P.M.—early afternoon. We can assume the crew had been up since 10 A.M. at the latest, preparing themselves and the aircraft for the flight.

The aircraft went first to Shannon, Ireland where it arrived at 1638. The crew was briefed and the aircraft fueled. At 1752 the flight departed Shannon and arrived at Keflavik, Iceland at approximately 2000 hours Greenwich.

Those of you who have fueled and briefed at Keflavik know it's a cold and trying stop, particularly in February. After about an hour, the crew was ready to depart. Engines were started at 2113, but for some reason which the investigators could not discover, takeoff did not occur until 2131—18 minutes later. We suspect the crew was programming onboard navigation equipment.

By that time, the crew had been up and on the go for at least 10 hours; the flight had already been seven hours en route from Stuttgart.

The flight plan to Frobisher was via ALPHA, 64N/30W,

65N/40W, 65N/50W, 65N/60W, direct. The speed was to be 430 knots at FL390, time en route 2+58, fuel onboard 4+30, and the alternate was Sondrestrom, on the west coast of Greenland.

Readers who are familiar with the geography up in that area may be curious about the fuel reserve situation. In short, the crew was not legal because of the distance to an alternate, and the accident report lists this as one of the causes of the crash.

But can the crew be faulted on this point? Their route of flight took them just south of their alternate, Sondrestrom, at approximately 1+50 into the flight. Forecasts for both Sondrestrom and Frobisher called for scattered–to–broken conditions with a minimum ceiling of 1000 feet and good visibilities underneath.

The accident report doesn't say, but one can assume the crew was aware that the weather was holding better than forecast, although there were reports of patchy ice–crystal fog in the area of Frobisher. Since the captain had written in the flight log (recovered from the wreckage) that he anticipated having only 1420 pounds of fuel remaining on arrival at Frobisher, it is quite probable that he was following the frequently practiced procedure in business jets of filing for an alternate in reverse. He filed to Frobisher, but with an intermediate point as an alternate. He most likely intended to stop at his en route alternate if the Frobisher weather began to go sour or if headwinds were greater than forecast.

That sort of fuel planning is illegal, and no one can condone it. Still, it is widely practiced and very rarely leads to an accident. Had it not been compounded by a hard-luck string of other factors plus an error in basic judgment, it probably would not have resulted in tragedy this time.

The aircraft was equipped with a Global Navigation GNS-200 low frequency navigation system. This system depends on a string of U.S. Navy VLF communications stations for guidance. It is necessary to note that at the time of this accident the U.S.

Navy did not guarantee continuous operation of those stations *and in fact routinely pulled them off the air at 2300 to 2400 hours Greenwich for data updating.* Additionally, the U.S. FAA still does not approve VLF signals alone as the primary navigational aid.

Nevertheless, the crew was using the GNS–200 for track guidance. Whether or not they were aware that the stations might shut down *just minutes before their scheduled arrival at Frobisher* is unknown. That information was not made public by the Navy, so they probably did not. In any event, the use of this equipment, backed up with appropriate navigational alternatives, was, in 1974, accepted practice in both business and arctic flying. In our estimation, the crew cannot be faulted on this point either.

Judging from the log entries, it is probable that the crew had weighed all of these factors before taking off from Keflavik at 2131. Military radar tracked the aircraft over Greenland and across the Davis Strait. This is a defense radar network, so position information is not normally passed on to either the crew or to ATC. Such information evidently was not given in this instance and there was no need to do so until shortly before the last plot, at 0012. For the first two hours and 14 minutes the flight proceeded normally against light headwinds (25 to 45 knots, which were close to those forecast), but it was slightly north of track. We have no way of knowing whether or not the crew realized they were off course; we know only that at 2345 the aircraft was abruptly turned approximately 20 degrees left, back toward the intended track of their flight.

A heading change that large is unnatural on this sort of flight unless there is some compelling reason for it. The Canadian MoT assumes the crew was following GNS–200 guidance. In our estimation that is not a safe assumption. This was an experienced crew, and one would not expect them to make a critical course correction based on a single nav aid. Did the crew run an ADF cross–check and decide it was more accurate than their GNS–200? Or did they plot a position visually while crossing Greenland and decide to put their faith in it? Either supposition is as good as assuming the crew blindly followed VLF information.

In any event, five minutes later, at 2350, the captain noted in his log that one VLF station (Maine) being used for track guidance had gone off the air. Two minutes later a second station (Washington) went off the air. Seven minutes later, at 2359, the captain recorded the loss of the final station, Great Britain, probably as the result of the Greenland icecap effect.

The crew had at this time, 2359, been on duty at least 10 and a half hours, and had been out of bed at least 12 hours. It was 10 at night in Stuttgart, where they had awakened that day; five in the morning at their homes in Toronto, where they had been only three days earlier. They'd had two quick turnarounds at Shannon and Keflavik, with probably not enough time for a hot meal at either place, and they still had well over a thousand miles to go before reaching home.

The Canadian report doesn't mention it, but fatigue must have played a large part in the events of the next 59 minutes.

In the first few minutes after 0000 GMT, the VLF stations began coming back on the air. The crew followed instructions in the GNS–200 manual for reacquiring track after station outages and recorded their actions in the aircraft log. During this time, however, the aircraft crossed through the flight planned track to Frobisher and maintained a course that would take it south of the airport. At 0012, when military radar recorded a final plot, the aircraft was still holding this course.

One can do a lot of guessing about that error in heading. The Canadian investigators imply that the VLF equipment may have been in error. Perhaps. But the captain was no novice. He may have figured that the course correction he had made at 2345—before the VLF outages—presumably with good reason, was more reliable than the reset GNS–200 indications. In that event, he would have held the course, expecting to begin receiving the Frobisher low frequency beacon at any instant.

That was good thinking under the circumstances, but unfortunately the Frobisher beacon was off the air. The station operator coming on duty at 0000 hours checked the transmitter and found that neither the primary nor the backup was sending out a signal. A technician was called, but the equipment was not declared operational until 0059. By that time the aircraft had crashed.

In addition to this beacon, Frobisher has an ILS with compass locators at both the outer and middle markers, plus DME. This equipment was operating normally during the period. On the date of the accident there was also an operating range station at Frobisher with an output of 400 watts. Since it was due to be decommissioned when a VOR facility was completed, information on it was not shown on Canadian charts. Nevertheless, local operators and overflying air carriers routinely used it for navigation. Evidently the crew of CF–BRL thought it was off the air, which would have been an honest assumption because a NOTAM issued six months earlier had stated it would be shut down in October 1973. Finally, there is a low frequency beacon on Brevoort Island, 120 miles east of Frobisher. The crew was aware of this last facility and eventually tried to use it, but by then it was too late.

So the crew arrived in the vicinity of Frobisher with the navigation situation in a state of high confusion. Let's look as closely as possible at what they did after that last radar plot at 0012.

At 0013 ATC cleared the flight for descent, *but did not mention the beacon outage.* At that moment, based on the flight plan, the crew would have assumed they were 16 minutes from Frobisher and making good a groundspeed of 400 knots; therefore they should have been about 100 miles east of the airport. Since the Sabre 40 manual shows that 120 miles and 19 minutes are re-

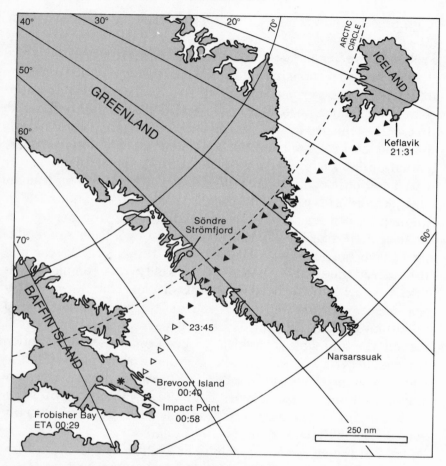

Sabreliner CF-BRL departed Keflavik at 2131 with an expected arrival time at Frobisher of 0029. Radar plots of the flight's progress appeared normal until 2345 when it abruptly turned south approximately 20 degrees. Five minutes later VLF nav stations were lost; 11 minutes after that the NDB at Frobisher was found to be off the air. So from 0001, navigation aids were inoperative or suspect—yet the crew began a descent at 0014. Why?

quired to descend from FL390, it was indeed time to start down. The crucial question is, should they have done so?

The answer must be an emphatic no. Working backward from the times and distances given in the accident report, we can see that at 0013 the aircraft was still no less than 140 and possibly as much as 180 miles east of Frobisher. Had the crew used one of the two ADFs onboard to cross–check the Brevoort Island beacon 120 nm east of Frobisher, they would have known they were not making good their estimated groundspeed. In that case, no experienced jet pilot would have started down. We must assume the crew failed to make that cross–check. At 0014 they reported beginning their descent. That decision was the fatal mistake.

At 0025 the flight called Frobisher and reported that neither the beacon nor the DME was being received. This should have alerted the crew to the extreme severity of the problem and caused them to climb back up to a more fuel efficient altitude to buy as much time as possible, but they did not. The descent was continued to an altitude so low that radio contact with Frobisher was lost. The last chance for survival vanished at that instant. The aircraft was then probably 85 to 90 miles—19 to 21 minutes at the 250 knots they would have been doing at low altitude—from Frobisher, and it was 33 minutes from flameout.

Within the next couple of minutes the crew finally remembered the beacon on Brevoort Island. It was tuned up on the number one ADF, and the evidence leads us to surmise that the crew back–tracked to that known point. If they were indeed 85 to 90 east of Frobisher at 0025, they would have been 30 to 35 west of Brevoort at that moment, which is eight to 12 minutes at 200 to 250 knots. Thus they should have arrived over Brevoort Island at 0033 to 0037.

According to the investigators, "At approximately 0040 a small jet aircraft, believed to be CF–BRL, was observed to circle once at low altitude (estimated 1500 feet) over the radio beacon at

Brevoort Island . . . and depart in the direction of Frobisher."

A map found in the wreckage indicates the crew drew a crude course to Frobisher from Brevoort Island and attempted to follow it, but tracked 18 miles south, to the left of this course.

At 0050 an overflying airline jet, at the request of Frobisher radio, contacted the crew, which reported being lost and at 4500 feet. The frequency of the soon–to–be decommissioned range station was relayed to them and was tuned up on the number two ADF. The crew reported turning toward the station.

The fuel warning lights were on and the crew, which showed considerable professionalism to the end, told the seven passengers to prepare for a crash landing. At 0056 the crew told the airline flight overhead that they were going down. At 0058, 3+37 after departing Keflavik, the aircraft impacted the side of a small hill at 2080 feet msl, and all nine onboard died instantly.

In reviewing the events leading up to this accident one might conclude the crew was victimized by the failure of ground–based navigation aids. We do not believe this, however. There were, in our view, six contributing causes, capped by one error in judgment.

• Departing Keflavik with an expected reserve at Frobisher of only 1420 pounds was not wise. This was compounded by a hold of 18 minutes on the ground at Keflavik for some unknown reason. The hold would have consumed 200 or less pounds, but with a mere 1420 pounds in reserve, the crew should have shut down and topped off before departing. We suspect they did not because of the uncomfortable conditions on that ramp at Keflavik and because of their fatigue. In spite of that decision, the crew had sufficient fuel to complete the flight, the radio outages notwithstanding.

• The shutdown of the VLF stations was crucial, but the crew had several options in overcoming that problem. It is fundamental that you don't rely on a single navigation method on any flight, particularly in the hostile northern part of the world. There are numerous radio beacons up there that can be used to plot a position. And the flight *was* in radar contact. These are defense radars and the military doesn't like to become involved in ATC services, but certainly they can and will help in an emergency. Several years ago, I elicited position reports from them, and they were quite accommodating.

• Failure of the Frobisher beacon was also crucial, but again the crew had at least one alternative. Why they did not tune in the Brevoort Island beacon sooner—or whether they did and failed to use the information wisely—will never be known. If the aircraft had been equipped with a cockpit voice recorder, we would undoubtedly learn much more about accident avoidance and prevention from this incident.

• The failure of the Frobisher controller to notify the crew of the beacon outage is unconscionable. ATC personnel, including technicians, should not for an instant forget what their central purpose is—guidance of aircraft. Had the man who discovered this outage instantly caused a NOTAM to be broadcast on all available frequencies, this accident would probably not have occurred. The crew was not blameless in this regard, however. Anytime you think you should be receiving a navigational aid and aren't, you should start asking questions of everyone within hailing distance. Why the crew neglected to ask Frobisher about their not being able to receive the beacon earlier is another of the unknowns in the accident.

• Fatigue, we suspect, was a primary cause of this accident. Several things the crew did were totally uncharacteristic of men who have flown a lot in the far north: The 18–minute delay on the ground at Keflavik with engines running, the abrupt change in course 44 minutes prior to their Frobisher estimate, the failure to cross–check Brevoort Island NDB for position. Anyone who has flown this route knows it's a tense undertaking at best. Add to that the bitter cold of a couple of refueling stops, the lack of time to relax with a hot meal and the darkness, and the situation becomes too much. Eight hours continuous duty and one en-route stop between rest periods should be the limit required of any crew conducting a critical flight like this one.

• The crew's decision to start down without a certain knowledge of their position was the fatal stroke. When you have a fuel problem in any airplane, the three Cs must be followed: climb, conserve, communicate. All of the above problems and a couple more could have been overcome with relative ease had the crew stayed at FL390 until they were receiving their destination fix and knew precisely where they were. On a time and distance basis they should have been 100 miles from their destination when they elected to descend. The fact that they were receiving neither the beacon nor DME information should have told them they weren't as close to Frobisher as they thought they were. When they began that descent, they probably had 1100 to 1200 pounds remaining. That's my estimate, using the Sabre 40 flight manual and figuring backwards from actual flameout. According to the charts in the manual, that much fuel would have kept them aloft at least another hour and taken them at least 440 nm. Starting down too early is a small error. We all make it often. But again, aviation is terribly unforgiving of errors. You can make a couple and get away with them—or three or four stacked on top of one another. But when you get to five and six, something is certain to break.

THREE TOOLS FOR IMPROVING SAFETY

3

Radar, shoulder harnesses, and cockpit voice–recorders have much in common when the subject is safety.

Radar as a Terrain-Avoidance Tool (March 1978)

In our discussion of the crash of a Sabreliner near Frobisher in the Canadian Northwest, we spoke at length about navigational facilities that failed, crew fatigue, the necessity to stay high in a jet until you're certain where you are, and the proper use of an ADF. But we failed to mention that had the crew used their airborne radar properly, nine deaths might have been prevented.

Briefly, the situation was this: The crew was flying the Sabre 40 from Iceland to Frobisher with seven businessmen passengers onboard. Although they were low on fuel and weren't receiving any of the Frobisher navigational aids, they commenced a descent evidently based on time versus estimated groundspeed. Again evidently, their estimated position was in error. They were farther out than they thought. They became lost at low altitude and ran out of fuel before getting the navigational situation straightened out.

They had all sorts of navigational equipment onboard, including a VLF system, so it probably never occurred to them to back it all up with their airborne radar.

But they had crossed two coasts and were approaching a third when they began the descent. If they'd turned their radar on and tilted the antenna down, they could have made a precise ground-speed check when crossing the east and west coasts of Greenland and when making landfall at Baffin Island. They also would have known exactly their distance from, and their approximate position relative to Frobisher.

Just two years later, in January 1976, an FAA crew made a similar error over the South Atlantic. In that case, too, if the crew had used the mapping feature of their on-board radar, they probably could have made a landfall and avoided a ditching that resulted in the death of one of the three crewmembers.

There is a critical lesson in those two accidents for every pilot who flies behind radar. We've become so used to always knowing where we are to a tenth of a mile by other means, that we've come to treat the ground–mapping capability of weather radar as a mere novelty. In fact, however, the radar can be a lifesaving navigational backup to the other electronics on the panel, and it's easy to use. More on that later.

There have been several similar accidents: A World Airways DC–8 at Cold Bay, Alaska; a Texas International Convair 600 at Mena, Arkansas; a TWA 727 at Dulles; a Learjet at Palm Springs; and a Cessna 421 at Nogales, Arizona; a Falcon 20 and a Learjet in Mexico; a Convair near Bishop, California; and a United DC–8 near Salt Lake City. The common thread in all those accidents was that the aircraft involved slammed into a mountain.

None of those accidents would have occurred had the crews been using their weather radar for terrain avoidance.

30

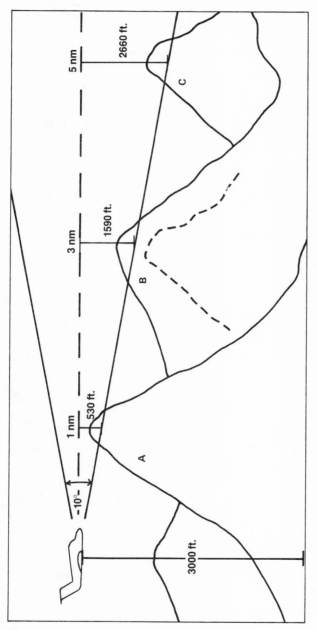

To use weather radar for terrain avoidance you must first fly low across some peaks to discover how to adjust your particular system. You'll find the gain must be turned way down to eliminate a side-lobe problem. But once you learn how, the relationship depicted here will hold true. For every mile the indicator shows there's terrain ahead, figure you'll miss it by no more than 500 feet—*if at all.*

Amazingly, many pilots who have flown thousands of hours behind radar have never thought about using it to warn them of high terrain ahead. Many of them will even argue long and loud that airborne radar *can't* be used for terrain avoidance.

It can. To prove it, we worked up the diagram shown here, then went out in a radar-equipped Aztec and flew back and forth over a prominent peak. Sure enough, the radar indicated precisely by how much we would clear the peak and when we weren't going to clear it.

Let's study Figure 3 carefully. The theory is simple: A radar pulse goes out in an expanding beam. In order to look at weather, the beam needs to be as narrow horizontally as possible, so the antenna is designed to squeeze in the sides of the cone–shaped beam. The result is a beam that is typically five degrees wide by 10 degrees up and down. Those dimensions will vary from about three degrees by seven degrees to about 10 degrees by 15 degrees, depending on the antenna–dish size. But for terrain–avoidance purposes, 10 degrees up and down or five degrees above and below the aiming point is a good starting assumption.

With that assumption and a bit of basic trigonometry it's possible to predict the height of those mountain peaks up ahead. Suppose you're flying level, with the radar set on zero tilt and painting terrain five miles ahead: By triangulation, you can be certain you'll top that peak by 2660 feet—or less. That *or less* is important. You can't be certain how *much* less, but you can be certain that you're not going to clear the peak by any *more than* 2660 feet—*if at all.*

If the peak is still showing on the radar at three miles, you'll top it by 1590 feet *or less.* Assuming that peak C is 500 feet high (the airplane is at 3000), notice what happens when it's three miles distant, as depicted by the dashed resemblance. It has slid under the beam coverage and will have disappeared from the radar display.

32

The situation relative to peak A is terrifying. With the radar set up like this, if a peak is showing at one mile, it's probably the end, because you'll top it by 530 feet, *or less.*

From this example, we can derive a rule of thumb: If terrain is showing at five miles with the radar tilt adjusted to the horizon, watch out. If it's still there at three miles, climb like hell.

Note also that the ratio is about 500 feet per mile. If terrain is showing at 10 nm, you'll pass over it at 5000 feet, *or less;* at 20 nm you'll top it at 10,000 feet, *or less.* That's good knowledge to have in hand just before commencing an approach. If in hilly or mountainous country you have a ground target at 10 nm with zero tilt on the antenna, you obviously don't want to descend more than 3000 feet within the next 10 miles.

Since the radar beam spreads out five degrees from centerline, you may wonder why we don't recommend using five degrees of uptilt. That way if nothing is shown, you're safe.

But don't try it. You can't be certain the antenna is level. With an unstabilized system it will follow the attitude of the aircraft. Even with a stabilized system, you can't be certain it's accurate to a degree. Therefore, strive to point the beam precisely along the flight path, so you'll have a five–degree margin for antenna–tilt error.

What happens in a climb or descent? Take the case of the unstabilized antenna first: In most prop aircraft the rule of thumb —target at five miles, look out; at three miles, climb like hell—will generally hold true in the descent if the indicated airspeed remains about the same. The relative body attitude in aircraft that use unstabilized antennas changes very little between cruise and descent. In a climb, gear and flaps up, the antenna should be tilted down about three degrees. These aircraft tend to climb at an angle of three to four degrees at lower elevations with a pitch attitude of five to 10 degrees.

The pitch attitude of most jets will vary quite a lot between

33

cruise and departure or descent speeds, but most jets also have stabilized antenna systems.

In the case of a stabilized antenna, the tilt control should be adjusted just the reverse of that used for a manual system. While climbing, leave the control at zero–degree tilt. That'll result in about an extra three–degree safety margin, but in the climb, a little extra margin is welcome. For descent, the tilt control for a stabilized antenna should be turned *down* about three degrees. Most descents work out to about three degrees, so a three–degree down angle on a stabilized antenna will restore the normal safety margin.

So much for theory. In the real world, you'll find that the shortest range on many older radars is 20 or 30 miles. That makes reading out distances down to three or five miles difficult. Also, the side–lobe suppression on many older radars is poor, so you'll get ghost images from terrain that is well below you. Nevertheless, with experimentation and practice on clear days, you'll find that even older radars will provide some terrain warning.

Most of the newer digital radars will range down to five to 10 miles. That's good—and something to be considered when selecting a system. In any case, however, practice is required. The first thing you'll discover is that you must turn the gain down. The poorer the side–lobe suppression, the more the gain must be decreased to yield a paint of only the desired terrain.

If you're having to worry about both thunderstorms and high terrain, your radar skills must be even sharper. Switching back and forth between the weather and map modes will help, but keep your mind on that gain. It can get you into trouble if it's not where you want it when you're alternatively looking for heavy rain and rocks.

We hope you're now convinced about this technique. If not, next time you fly in and out of a mountainous area, try it. You'll be surprised. Also, learn to use your radar for normal, down–

looking mapping and do some creative thinking about how it can be a cross–check on your usual navigational equipment.

In a sense, all this is a freebie from your radar, yours for the price of a bit of practice. And it can be an extremely valuable freebie.

Shoulder Harnesses Are a Nuisance . . . But the Alternative Is So Final (December 1973)

Both pilots probably could have survived if they had worn shoulder harnesses. —NTSB

Back in 1973, the NTSB sent a safety recommendation to the FAA that made its cause–and–circumstance point with unmistakeable clarity.

"On February 21, 1973, a Learjet crashed at Willow Run Airport, Ypsilanti, Michigan. Although the cockpit remained structurally intact, both crewmembers died as a result of loss of restraint when their seatbelts failed at the outboard attach points. Our investigation disclosed that shoulder harnesses not only would have redistributed the forces applied to the seatbelts, thereby reducing the possibility of failure, but also would have prevented violent upper torso movement, thereby alleviating the crewmembers' injuries."

As a result of that finding—plus a long history of unnecessary deaths because shoulder harnesses either weren't available or weren't worn—the NTSB asked the FAA to amend Parts 121 and 91 to bring air carrier aircraft manufactured before January 1, 1958 under the appropriate regulations, and to include all Part 25 airplanes operated under Part 91 in the new regulations on shoulder harness installation and use.

To that we say *bravo*. Just why corporate jets were left out of the amendments to FAR 91 requiring shoulder harnesses on all

35

smaller aircraft (NPRM 73–1) is something only the FAA can answer. It seems obvious that saving the lives of corporate crews and passengers is as important as saving the lives of people in Cherokees and Cessna 172s.

Although there has been some spirited discussion about the requirement for shoulder harnesses in the passenger compartment (some safety engineers maintain that the same end can be achieved by delethelization techniques), virtually all the safety people agree that upper torso restraint systems in the cockpit are desirable.

Unfortunately, not all pilots agree, nor do all pilots wear the harnesses that are installed. Their reasons are discomfort, fear that the system might prevent them from reaching a vital control at a vital moment, and just plain I–don'–wanna–be–bothered. There's not much anyone can do about the last, except to note that the animal famous for refusing to drink after being led to water is first cousin to a jackass.

The other two reasons are legitimate, but there is hardware readily available to take care of them. Inertial reels, for example, ready for installation in anything from a J–3 to a G–II, can be purchased off–the–shelf. I've had a set in my own airplane for the past 2500 hours and not once have they kept me from reaching a control. Even if the reel locks up, everything vital is within reach.

Admittedly, the single strap inertial system isn't the most comfortable. Nevertheless, we keep the harness in place at all times to preclude the possibility of sudden pilot or copilot incapacitation leading to an accident. There is at least one instance on record of this happening in a U.S. air carrier operation. The captain of a Lockheed Electra had a heart attack during a circling approach and the copilot, who was looking out his side window at the airport when the captain suddenly slumped over the controls, wasn't able to get the inert body off the yoke and pull up before hitting a hill.

Evidently this possibility is recognized as a real threat by European airlines, several of which have installed special shoulder harness systems that automatically lock at critical times in a flight and unlock at other times to give the crew full freedom. In some installations the reels are locked whenever the gear is down, in others whenever the flaps are out, and in still others whenever the no–smoking/seatbelt signs are lighted. This arrangement answers both the comfort and restricted–movement arguments. We hope we'll see it offered before too long in business airplanes.

With sophisticated technology to help us, shoulder harnesses are going to be much less of a nuisance in our airplanes than in our cars.

If we're smart, we'll think about that and buckle up cheerfully on each flight—because the NTSB epitaph quoted above is long overdue for extinction.

Are We Ready For Cockpit Voice Recorders? (May 1974)

I don't know about you, but mysterious crashes make me nervous. If only there had been a cockpit voice recorder onboard to reveal more of what was happening, how much more we would know that might prevent future accidents.

CVRs for private aircraft is a great idea. Each year there are 30 to 35 crashes, according to my reckoning, for which there will never be reliable causes listed. Just offhand I can count nine pairs in which an early understanding of the cause of the first accident in the pair might have prevented the second. In every case, if only we had known what the crew had been talking about just before impact, and if we could have heard the sounds of switches and controls being manipulated, we could have estimated the cause quite accurately.

Listen—so to speak—to this:

COPILOT: All right . . . well, twenty one hundred feet at seven mi . . . .

(Sound of two rapid clicks.)

CAPTAIN: All right.

UNKNOWN: What was it?

CAPTAIN: Pitch light, huh?

COPILOT: Yeah.

(Sound of click.)

CAPTAIN: Watch the TGT on that side.

COPILOT: Yeah, okay. First time I've ever seen that.

(Sound of three or four clicks. Sound similar to levers being actuated twice.)

COPILOT: And a little bit right.

CAPTAIN: Right, of course.

COPILOT: Yeah . . . and . . . we're approaching fourteen hundred feet.

CAPTAIN: I don't know whether it came out of it. We'll leave it right there.

COPILOT: Yeah. *(Pause)* You mean it won't go, ah, any further than that right now, Rusty?

CAPTAIN: No.

COPILOT: Is that right? Oh boy.

(Sound of two clicks.)

COPILOT: Want me to advise maintenance, or, ah, ah, oops, oh, I mean Albany.

CAPTAIN: Yeah.

COPILOT: What do you want me to tell 'em?

CAPTAIN: Tell 'em we have, ah . . . prop hung up on . . . cruise pitch lock.

COPILOT: Okay. *(Copilot advises maintenance the left engine is "hung up on the locks." Maintenance evidently does not fully understand and responds, "Yeah, your left engine—there's somethin' the matter with it. Okay.")*

CAPTAIN: Better shut it down.

COPILOT: You gotta . . . . You gotta shut it down?

CAPTAIN: Do you see the runway out there?

COPILOT: No, not yet . . . not yet. We're a little bit right.

(Sound of three clicks.)

CAPTAIN: Tell 'em we got a problem.

COPILOT: Okay.

(Sound of engine spool down and copilot tells approach, "We're feathering our, ah, left engine. We have a problem there." More sound of spool down and clicks.)

CAPTAIN: Give me an inch on the pedal.

COPILOT: Huh?

CAPTAIN: Didn't . . . get it to feather! See if you can.

COPILOT: Okay.

(Sound of several clicks.)

CAPTAIN: Tell 'em we're gonna land short, we're in trouble.

(Sound of clicks and copilot tells approach, "Ah, four-oh-five's gonna land short. We're in trouble.")

UNIDENTIFIED: No chance!

UNIDENTIFIED: I'm a *.

End of recording.

Notice that nothing went out on the air from the flight that really told anyone outside the aircraft what the problem was. After listening to the cockpit recording, however, the problem— a prop hangup—and what the crew tried to do about it—and failed to do—is very evident.

If we had that kind of information from every business aviation crash, we could make tremendous gains in our safety record over the next few years. How can we get it? Why not voluntarily install CVRs in our airplanes?

39

That idea may turn a lot of pilots and crews off for a variety of reasons. The first objection would be cost. We've done some checking and have discovered that units are available for around $2000. That's not bad for turbine equipment and even the quarter–million dollar twins, but for little guys it's a bit steep. Further checking indicates we could probably put CVRs onboard for as little as $300—assuming the FAA will look the other way and let us make an adequate installation rather than a gold–plated one. All we really need is a little $89 recorder with a continuous cartridge in it. A secondary power source would be nice, but so few accidents result from total electrical failure that it would probably not be cost effective. We don't even need elaborate shock protection, because all we want to survive is the tape itself. That would require only that the package be thermally encapsulated. Actually, thermal protection may not be necessary, because in 90 percent of our accidents the tail of the aircraft survives. If the unit were mounted way back there, it would need little protection of any sort.

A second objection might be that pilots would be inhibited from speaking out if they knew a recorder was on. That hasn't been a problem in air carriers. Evidently, the it'll–never–happen–to–me syndrome overcomes inhibitions.

A third objection might be that the boss could use the tape to spy on the crew. That's silly. Since the tape rerecords on itself each half hour, all the crew has to do is behave during the final 30 minutes before shutdown and there'll never be anything on the tape to get anyone in trouble.

A fourth and perhaps the most valid objection is that the guys who most ought to have a CVR in their planes would be the least likely to put one in voluntarily. To be cost effective, at least 15,000 aircraft should be equipped. Whether or not it's necessary to have a representative portion of them in airplanes flown by poorly trained, undisciplined pilots could be the subject of a heated hangar session. It's likely that a study would disclose that when a poor or careless pilot bends an airplane the cause is apparent. It's when a good pilot or crew racks one up for no discernable reason that we should all become nervous and want to know what the cause was. Therefore, even if just the conscientious pilots and aircraft owners installed CVRs, we would gain much valuable information.

THE APPROACH 4

Among experienced, instrument–rated pilots, the approach phase of flight has proved to be by far the time of greatest danger. There are *mathematical* reasons for that being so.

The Miracle Mile (August 1972)

The nonprecision approach has been the subject of so many articles, and so many National Transportation Safety Board reports, rule changes and even Congressional investigations, one would think that whatever can be said about it has already been said.

The startling fact, however, is that hardly anyone has dared to point out that under the present FAA criteria for setting minimums, the safe execution of most nonprecision approaches in medium and heavy turbine aircraft is mathematically improbable, if not impossible. Even in light twins and heavy singles it's a dangerous maneuver.

Pilots of heavy equipment know this intuitively. Smart ones never push the odds; the ones who think they are clever try to compensate in devious ways and too often end up in the NTSB record book.

Why is the nonprecision approach so dangerous? It's a matter of elementary trigonometry. As an example, consider the nonprecision approach to minimums of 500 and one when the visibility actually is one mile. Recalling the profile of a standard nonprecision approach and remembering that visibility is given in statute miles (5280 feet per mile), here's what happens:

After crossing the fix and descending to the MDA of 500 feet above the threshold, the aircraft is leveled off and the speed stabilized at, say 130 knots (219.4 feet per second), the crew then begins looking for the runway. At exactly one mile, 5280 feet eyeball to threshold, the first officer calls the runway in sight.

In terms of time alone, the captain is then faced with a most difficult task. In just 24 seconds he must transition from straight-and-level flight on instruments to a visual descent of at least 1250 fpm, pick up any misalignment (this is a nonprecision approach, remember), arrest the high rate of sink, and plant the mains on the numbers. Only 24 seconds is not much time to accomplish all that when one has 10,000 to 30,000 pounds of machinery strapped to one's backside.

The eye–opener, though, is in the triangulation. Assuming the captain isn't super–human, at least four seconds will be lost in looking up from the instruments, identifying the runway and establishing a descent. In that time the aircraft will travel 878 feet, so the final descent will begin only 4378 horizontal feet from the threshold. That results in an approach angle of more than 6.5 degrees and a final rate of descent of 1500 fpm.

In a semi–STOL turboprop, that may not be so bad, but in a turbojet . . . in poor visibility . . . to a wet runway?

Obviously, the higher the MDA, the steeper the approach. For instance, if you've often wondered why you always land hard and never seem to have enough brakes after a backcourse 33 approach to minimums at Detroit City Airport, it's because the approach angle is greater than 7.5 degrees and the final rate of descent to get on the runway, after spotting it when only a mile out, is 1930 fpm.

At 400 and one you have a better chance of getting on with something less than a crunch, but not much. At 400 and one, the angle of approach must be just over 5.5 degrees and the final rate of descent must be 1200 fpm.

NTSB files are full of reports of turbojet pilots who have come to grief trying to land out of approaches that are too steep. The classic involved a 727 captain approaching Salt Lake City some years ago; he drove the landing gear through the wings.

To elude that fate, some pilots routinely leave the MDA for a lower altitude whenever they have ground contact and a mile visibility even though they do not have the actual runway in sight. Perhaps this is a holdover from fledgling days in slow trainers, in which a mile visibility is legal VFR. Whatever their rationale, the NTSB's records of what has happened to many of them over the past few years can fill a closet.

Thus far we've addressed only the straight–in mathematics. Circling approaches are something else entirely. Think about this: Visibility minimums for a circling approach in Category C airplanes (121 knots or greater) are normally increased 50 percent over straight–in approaches to 1.5 miles. But in a standard–rate turn at 130 knots (which is a mite slow for a standard–rate turn in many turbojets), a horizontal distance of 8385 feet is needed to turn 180 degrees. That's 465 feet *more* than 1.5 statute miles. To circle to a runway in 1.5–mile visibility, therefore, and to keep the runway in sight as required in Advisory Circular 61–72B, the turbojet pilot must turn a little bit tighter than standard rate and (assuming a 180–degree side approach) must enter the turn abeam the threshold and roll out just prior to touchdown. To do that, it's necessary to descend in the turn. Starting at 500 feet agl, the average rate of descent must be just over 500 fpm through the approach. This leads to some grim heights above the threshold at some frightening positions relative to the runway. Either that or a rate of sink of 1000 fpm during the final 90 degrees of turn to

44

the runway is required. The consequences of such calculations are on file at the NTSB.

Is the FAA aware of these computations? Yes. Internal reports have been filed calling attention to them. The FAA is not yet disposed to changing TERPS criteria, but turbojet pilots can and should devise their own procedures to insure that they don't get bitten by a tangent or cosine.

Whether from direct knowledge of the mathematics or by intuition, most experienced turbine crews forget about reported visibilities once it has been determined that they may legally commence a nonprecision approach. Visibilities at most non–ILS–equipped airports are really meaningless anyway, because what a Flight Service Station specialist sees from the FSS steps and what a pilot sees from the cockpit are two different worlds.

Time is the significant factor in a nonprecision approach. If the pilot has time to position his aircraft 200 feet above the threshold altitude at a point one–half mile from the numbers (which corresponds to the height at the middle marker on a full ILS approach), he can land it safely. An attempted landing becomes increasingly risky if this position must be compromised. At 130 knots, the one–half mile point comes only 12 seconds after spotting the runway in one–mile visibility. The time necessary to position the aircraft after picking up the runway varies with the aircraft type, the presence or absence of VASI and the skill of the crew, but it cannot safely be more than six seconds per 100 feet of altitude above the 200 feet desired, plus five seconds for recognition and transition to visual flight. Even that results in a descent of 1000 fpm to the half–mile point, which should be the absolute maximum in poor visibility. Therefore, 23 seconds are needed to spot the runway from an altitude of 500 feet agl and maneuver to the proper position for landing. Since in one–mile visibility, only 12 seconds are available at 130 knots, it becomes clear why so many turboprops and jets are involved in nonprecision approach accidents.

If the MDA is 500 feet above the threshold and the aircraft is approaching at 130 knots, the runway must be in sight 35 seconds prior to the MAP if the final segment of the approach and landing are to be made with acceptable safety. Coincidentally, the visibility necessary is just under 1.5 miles. At an MDA of 600 feet above threshold, the time is 41 seconds and the required visibility is more than 1.75 miles.

That's something to think about the next time you're cleared for the approach and told it's 500 and one. It explains why the right hand of a grizzled old pro begins to twitch the throttles forward when the second hand on his clock indicates he still has a full three–quarters of a minute to go until MAP.

Ducking Under (November 1973)

Those of us who read accident reports carefully can tell when autumn has arrived. Along about Halloween each year we begin to see reports like this: "Approximately one mile from the runway threshold, Flight 105 struck trees and power lines at an elevation of 715 feet msl—85 feet agl."

As certainly as winter brings snow and crosswinds, that kind of report will continue to come in—two or three per month—from October until the first thunderstorm of spring. And, interestingly, those accident reports will be about pilots with several thousands of hours in their logs. This is not a novice's type of accident.

Of all the mysteries in aviation, this one is the most profound because the explanation for why it happens is so easy to grasp, even the dullest dolt cannot miss it.

The accompanying illustration shows a typical nonprecision approach. In the classic case, the crew is either vectored or flies a procedure turn to arrive over a Final Approach Fix. After crossing the FAF, the procedure calls for a descent to MDA, after

46

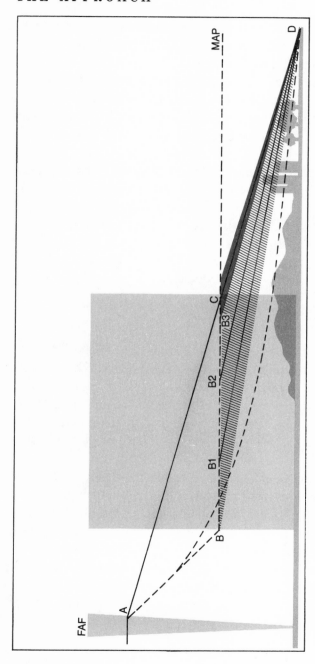

The ideal nonprecision approach profile is A direct to D, but most of us fly them A to B (which is the Minimum Descent Altitude) to D, more or less via C, which can put us into the obstacles if we misjudge the narrow descent window at C.

which (if the airport is not in sight), the aircraft is leveled off and flown at the MDA until the time–to–MAP has transpired. At that time a missed approach must be executed.

The inference from the rule (FAR 91.117) is that if the airport, or "markings identifiable with the approach end of that runway," is sighted at any time before the MAP is reached, the crew can descend from the MDA for landing.

That's what causes the problem; it just isn't so.

Look at the illustration again. Upon reaching the FAF, the crew has two options: Option one is that a rate of descent can be set up, based on time–to–MAP, that will result in the aircraft's going straight down the line ACD to the touchdown zone. Few of us do that, though, because if the wind plays tricks, we might break out above the line ACD and be too high to land. In addition, that procedure requires a split–second decision at point C. If the airport is in sight, we continue the approach; if not, we must instantly arrest the descent and go around.

Therefore we elect to follow option two.

In option two we throw out the gear and flaps at the FAF and descend quickly—as along line AB—to the MDA. This is safe because the folks who design approaches always give us obstruction clearance from the FAF to MAP if we are at or above MDA. Option two gives us the time between B and MAP to look the situation over and make a yea–or–nay decision, which is another reason we all prefer it.

In really bad weather this works out fine. We seldom see the runway or its environs before C, so the final descent is along CD and above obstructions. But now comes winter when, instead of heavy haze and blinding rain, the weather problem is low stratus, often with good visibility below.

See what happens? We descend from solid instruments at the FAF, break out into relatively good visibility somewhere between A and B, and see the runway or approach lights right away. If

48

VASI is not installed, the overpowering tendency is to continue the descent toward touchdown—and that's what gets us.

As you can see by the lines from B1, B2 and B3, there may be high terrain, buildings and trees on the direct line to the runway if MDA is left before C. Quite often this is compounded by our slowness in picking up the high sink rate developed between A and B (Why hurry? We're VFR and everything looks rosy), which results in a curved approach with a very flat final.

The cure is as simple as two plus two: Don't leave the MDA before C—not even when it's so clear underneath the overcast that you can see into next week.

Unfortunately—and to their shame—the approach–chart makers are of absolutely no help in telling us where C is. On the bottom of the approach plates we are given the time from the FAF to MAP at various airspeeds, which is useless information. Unless the airplane can descend vertically, the *real* MAP is at C. Since after passing C the angle to the touchdown zone becomes progressively steeper, flying the path between C and the MAP at MDA serves only to set us up for one of another pair of accident types —either the dive–for–it splat or the screeching overshoot. Moreover, dragging up from C to the MAP at the minimum descent altitude robs us of time and distance that could be better used in executing a missed approach.

Where *is* C? Obviously it varies with the MDA. (Purists will argue that it varies with the MDA, the speed *and* the maximum angle at which the aircraft is capable of approaching the runway. That is fine for purists but of little help to a pilot approaching a wet, icy runway in a crosswind.) My rule of thumb for business aircraft (approach speeds of 80 to 140 knots), is that C, expressed in seconds before MAP, is 10 percent of the published minimum altitude (HAT), minus three. For example, if the MDA is 500 feet above the touchdown zone, then C is at the time–to–MAP (as published at the bottom of the approach plate) less 47 seconds. (Ten percent of 500 is 50, minus three is 47.)

Trigonometry buffs will find that this results in an approach angle that runs from 2.5 to three degrees for turbine equipment and about 4.7 degrees for single–engine airplanes approaching at 80 knots. This is well within the capabilities of aircraft in those categories.

The rule of thumb, to be sure, is good only when there is a final approach fix off the airport by a couple of miles or more, either over a VOR or NDB, or by DME or radar position. When the approach facility is on the airport and no other position information is available, visibility minimums are normally higher, which makes judging the approach angle a bit more certain.

The FAA has long been saying that eventually an electronic descent fix will be established for all nonprecision approaches. That, VASI and/or one of the nonprecision approach computers on the market will someday eliminate this kind of accident. Until then, all we've got is an understanding of what causes the trouble and a rough rule of thumb to prevent it.

The Final Approach Accident (November 1975)

In a study of 94 accidents involving well–trained, proficient pilots, it was found that 27 percent of the mishaps occurred during the final descent to landing. That's highly significant when you consider that descent to landing accounts for only two percent, or two minutes, of the total flight time. This phase of flight accounted for 38 percent of the fatal accidents in the group and 30.5 percent of the deaths.

Obviously then, the final descent is a prime area for accident prevention. Therefore, let's take a look at each of the 25 final–descent accidents that occurred in one year among this group of professional and semi–professional pilots to see what they can teach us.

50

(1) January, in daylight——The pilot of a Cessna 421 collided with the ground while conducting an IFR approach to the Palm Springs, California airport. It was a single–pilot operation and the pilot was instrument rated with 2200 total hours. There were two passengers onboard. No one survived the crash.

The NTSB brief on the accident states only that the pilot conducted an improper or nonstandard IFR approach procedure. Officially the accident is listed, "Cause Unknown."

Without knowing exactly what happened, we cannot learn a specific lesson from this accident, but it should remind us all how important preplanning is in single–pilot operations. Procedures, altitudes, radials, and DME distances must be reviewed carefully, well before the approach begins. It's a good idea to also write headings, radials, and altitudes down in sequence, so they can be scratched out as the approach progresses. This is especially important when shooting an approach into a mountainous area like Palm Springs.

(2) January, in daylight——The pilot of a Cessna 320 landed long at Pensacola, Florida and ran through a ditch at the far end. The pilot had 1761 total hours.

The basic admonition to go around if you haven't touched down in the first third of the runway is too soon forgotten.

(3) January, in twilight——According to the NTSB brief, the crew of this King Air began a descent to an ILS approach at Blairstown, Iowa with insufficient time to descend to the approach altitude. The weather was 200 and a quarter in snow with reports of turbulence. The crew attempted to expedite the descent and the airplane broke up.

We have to do some guessing on this one, but it's possible that the captain was concerned about ice and decided to stay high as long as possible. He was an ATP with 4300 total hours. With that relatively low time, he may not yet have learned that you should never shoot an approach into weather you cannot fly out of. Stay-

51

ing high to avoid ice as long as possible may seem wise, but if there's too much ice to shoot a normal approach, there's probably too much to let you climb back out.

(4) February, in darkness and ice——A wing tip of a Cessna 340 hit the ground as the pilot was circling to land in VFR conditions at Fremont, Ohio. He misread or failed to read his altimeter. He was flying single pilot and had 2048 hours total, 581 in type.

(5) March, in twilight——An ATP with almost 12,000 total hours, 1200 of it in type, landed a Hansa Jet at Phoenix gear up. The NTSB report says it all: "Checklist—Failed to use."

(6) March, in darkness——The weather was 200 and a half in a thunderstorm. There is no ILS at Niles, Michigan, but the pilot of this Twin Comanche (single–pilot operation) attempted an approach there anyway. He descended below the MDA with fatal results. The remarkable thing is that this pilot had 16,770 total hours, 376 in type.

(7) March, in daylight——The pilot of an Aztec, flying alone, elected to land downwind at Snyder, Texas. He left 300 feet of skid marks on the far end of the runway.

(8) May, in daylight——The crosswind was gusting to 45, and the 4837–hour pilot (800 in type) was so preoccupied with that problem he forgot to lower the gear. "Checklist—Failed to use."

(9) May, in daylight——The captain of a Howard 500 landed downwind at Washington, Pennsylvania and hydroplaned off the end of the runway and down an embankment. He had 15,973 total hours, 780 in type.

(10) June, in daylight——The pilot had 6000 hours, 3000 in type. Flying an Aztec, he descended below the MDA at Princeton, Maine in rain and fog. The NTSB's brief comment: "Descended below MDA. Local weather conditions given to pilot by car–to–aircraft radio."

(11) June, in daylight——The "crew" of a Hughes 269A (We suspect that someone erred in charging this one to corporate/ex-

ecutive transportation) buzzed the airport and mushed out of the pullup. The machine was destroyed.

(12) June, in daylight——There must be a kind of madness in June. At Stanial Cay in the Bahamas, the pilot of an Aztec flew into the water during a low pass. He had 7500 total hours, 3896 in type.

(13) July, in daylight——Flying a Beech Duke, a commercial pilot with 1600 total hours, 60 in type, overshot an approach in 200 and one weather at Valdosta, Georgia. Instead of executing a missed approach, he attempted to circle and stalled out. This was a single–pilot operation. We charge this accident off to lack of experience. Since this was a nonprecision approach (localizer only) in 200 and one weather, the pilot obviously didn't recognize a missed approach when presented with one.

(14) August, in daylight——In a Cessna 185 on floats, the pilot (2400 hours; 40 in type) attempted to land in a canal that was too short.

(15) September, in daylight——The pilot of this Cessna 337 had 7000 total hours and 55 in type. He attempted a landing off–airport on wet, soft ground and wiped out the gear. There was a strip used by other aircraft a half–mile away.

(16) September, in daylight——The 3909–hour pilot attempted to land a Cessna 310 on an "airport recommended for use only by light single–engine aircraft." The gear collapsed in the ditches.

(17) October, in daylight——The pilot of a Cessna 421 (7400 hours total; 640 in type) selected the wrong runway at Tallahassee, Florida and lost control after touchdown.

The lesson here is to *always* determine the wind direction before each landing. It's amazing how many pilots don't. We once rode through a terrifying downwind landing on a short runway in a Sabreliner with an otherwise excellent ATP.

(18) October, in twilight——The pilot, who had 700 total hours and 55 in type, became preoccupied by the prospect of a night

landing and forgot about the gear of his Cardinal RG. A simple GUMP check would've prevented his embarrassment.

(19) October, in darkness——An Aztec pilot with 2414 hours, 143 in type, descended 1040 feet below the MDA during a localizer approach to Rochester, New York. He survived. He also blamed the altimeter for the accident, but it checked out—perhaps he had misread it. This also was a single–pilot operation, and the more of these accidents we study, the more convinced we are that single–pilot flying requires some kind of backup altitude warning device. The manufacturer who gives us a low–cost (under $1000) altitude alerter with voice annunciation is going to save a bunch of lives.

(20) November, in daylight——The pilot of a Falcon (7600 total hours; 2200 in type) touched down short at Galesburg, Illinois and wiped out the gear on the lip of the runway. He evidently didn't pay attention when one of his instructors was explaining that the landing distances shown in the charts allow for crossing the runway threshold at 50 feet. If it's necessary to touch down on the lip of a runway in order to get stopped on it, that runway is much too short.

(21) November, in darkness——The pilot had 860 total hours and only 10 in the Seneca he was flying, but he still attempted an approach at Memphis in 100 and one–half conditions, which were "slightly worse than forecast." He saw lights down through the fog and descended into trees three miles short of the runway.

(22) November, in darkness——En route to the old Greater Southwest Airport west of Dallas, the single pilot of a Cessna 310 experienced and reported to ATC a navigation receiver problem. After crossing the marker inbound, the aircraft was observed to turn left and descend into the ground, with fatal results to the pilot and his passenger. He had 23,903 hours, 500 in type, and was 65 years old. The radio problem may have been a factor, or it may have been pilot incapacitation.

(23) December, in darkness——The lone pilot of the Piper Twin

Comanche descended below the MDA at Walla Walla, Washington and proved with nauseating repetition that sooner or later busting minimums will get you. The pilot had 25,000 hours, 529 in type.

(24) December, in daylight——A King Air struck some trees during the approach to Columbia, South Carolina in 200 and three–quarters weather. It was a single–pilot operation (he had 6125 total hours; unknown in type), and the NTSB notes that pilot fatigue was a factor. The Board also notes that the weather was below minimums.

(25) December, in darkness——The unlighted runway at White Plains, New York was snow–covered, and the pilot of a Lear mistook the side for the center. He had 20,738 hours, 1231 in type. The damage to the airplane was substantial. If you insist on landing high–performance airplanes on unlighted, snow–covered runways, you've got to be prepared to take your lumps.

If the experiences of these 25 pilots teach you something, then their misfortunes will not have been a total waste. We hope you'll reread this list several times each year.

The "Homemade" Approach Procedure (July 1976)

Several years ago an acquaintance down in Texas developed a reputation for being able to deliver his air–taxi clientele to their destinations almost without fail. That is not remarkable except, coincidentally, his most frequent customer often was delivered to a country airport near Texarkana not served by an approach aid of any sort.

Our acquaintance had a system:—a homemade approach using a nearby broadcast station for guidance. It was a very formal procedure, with specified altitudes for each leg, an MDA, MAP, and even a missed approach turn back to the broadcast antenna.

The procedure worked well for him for years. He made a living using it, and his client's business in that small town eventually prospered to a point where the company could buy its own airplane, which the resourceful air–taxi pilot was hired to fly full time.

Within 60 days, the new airplane, the pilot, and his client were found scattered through the trees a mile short of that country airport.

What happened? The old story: It's one thing to push your luck to accommodate an air taxi client, quite another to push it when the only boss you've got is onboard. In the first instance, you can miss the approach and disappoint the client, knowing there are others to take his place if he stops using your services. But when the man in the back is The Boss—the only client you've got—the pressure is on. This ex–air taxi pilot simply busted his own minimums while trying to protect his job.

A similar story can be told about a homemade approach to an airport in Missouri, and another about one to an airport in Ohio. In each case the procedure was okay; it was a lack of adherence to it that caused a mishap.

Now the NTSB apparently has turned up a variation on that theme. In September of 1975, a Rockwell Turbo Commander 690A crashed on approach to the Nemacolin, Pennsylvania Airport. What is interesting about this mishap is the following quote from the NTSB report:

> During the investigation, the Safety Board obtained a copy of an unofficial and unapproved approach procedure for the Nemacolin Airport entitled, VFR safe altitude approach plate. The Safety Board could not determine who prepared the plate, but the investigation disclosed that aviation personnel of the [company] had access to the approach plate. Another pilot for the company stated he was reasonably sure that a copy of the approach plate was aboard N847CE when it crashed.
>
> The approach plate is constructed using the Indian Head VORTAC and its distance measuring equipment to establish

minimum safe altitudes below 5000 feet between the VOR-
TAC and Nemacolin Airport. The approach plate depicts a 226
degree radial from the Indian Head VORTAC; the instructions on the approach plate read as follows: "Conduct all
maneuvering NW of 226 IHD Radial when between 3400 feet
and 3800 feet msl." Additionally, the instructions state that
it should be used only in visual flight conditions.

The approach plate was not authorized by the FAA; there
are no authorized instrument approaches to the Nemacolin
Airport.

So, the crew evidently was conducting a homemade approach.
(Weather in the vicinity was 300 to 800 overcast with two–to–four
miles visibility.) The interesting part is that they were apparently
following the homemade approach to the letter. The aircraft disappeared from ATC radar about six miles southwest of Indian
Head VOR at an altitude of 2800 feet as reported by the encoding
altimeter. The wreckage was found on a ridge at an elevation of
2800 feet.

Mystery clouds the picture when one studies the homemade
approach plate that the crew apparently had. In a column on the
right side of the plate—headed, "Safe VFR Approach Altitudes to
Airport"—there was a notation that from the five–mile DME point
to "River Gorge" the safe altitude was 2800 feet. From "River
Gorge" the safe altitudes dropped on down to 2300 at the airport,
which is at 2000 feet msl.

Thus the encoder readout was accurate, so the altimeter was
properly set. The chart being used called out 2800 feet for the
aircraft's position and that's where it was, so the crew was reading the altimeters correctly. Still they hit the ridge.

Obviously, their chart was in error. Incredibly, the NTSB never
notes this fact in the report. The probable cause of the accident,
the Board says, "was the pilot's attempt to execute a VFR approach in meteorological conditions which precluded visual flight

to an airport which did not have an FAA–approved instrument approach procedure."

Evidently (and all this assumes, of course, that the NTSB's own data is accurate), the *actual* cause was that the crew was conducting an unauthorized IFR approach using an inaccurate, homemade approach plate.

We're not sure what the moral is here, but "Don't shoot homemade approaches" seems apt. Without condoning that practice, though, it must be observed that the use of an unauthorized approach was not the cause of this accident any more than the homemade approach caused the demise of our acquaintance in Texas.

There are two lessons to be learned from all of this: First, one shouldn't shoot bootleg approaches—*ever.* The danger seems not to stem from the approach itself—the FAA's ability (as opposed to authority) to devise an approach is neither divine nor exclusive —but from an *attitude* that cannot be separated from the *act.* Since the approach is illegal from start to finish, adherence to minimums also tends to be a bit wishy–washy. It's a case of the man who set the minimums having a right to alter them at his whim.

Second, if you *must* shoot a homemade approach, make sure the procedure is accurate. The NTSB notes that it wasn't able to determine who devised the approach that the crew of this 690 was using. Logic tells us, however, that it was not the crew. If they had devised it, a prerequisite to drawing up the approach would have been to fly it very attentively in VFR conditions before shooting it in IMC.

At least, if I were going to shoot a homemade approach, that's what I'd do.

HOW LOW NOT TO GO

5

Except for the inflight collision, virtually all
fatal accidents today occur because the
aircraft struck the ground. It is incumbent
on the airman, therefore, to think long
and thoroughly about how low he *can*
safely go.

MSA Awareness (February 1975)

It's tragic how bumbling and slow we sometimes are in learning
from the mistakes of others. In September 1973, a World Airways
cargo flight crashed into the side of Mount Dutton, 18 nm east of
Cold Bay, Alaska, after having been cleared for the approach
while still at FL310 and 125 DME from the airport.

Incredibly, the NTSB stumbled all around the real cause of the
accident and never pinpointed it. The official NTSB–designated
probable cause was "the captain's deviation from approved instrument approach procedures. As a result of the deviation, the flight
descended into an area of unreliable navigation signals and ob-
structing terrain."

In short, the captain got too low and hit a mountain—which was pretty apparent before the investigation began. The real question is, *why* did he get too low?

The answer did not come to light until after a TWA 727 smashed into another mountain, northwest of Dulles, in December 1974. Seconds before impact, someone in the crew (possibly the second officer) questioned the captain about his descent from the last assigned altitude to 1800, the initial approach altitude. He replied that they'd been cleared for the approach and therefore for a descent to the initial approach altitude.

There's the answer to the vital question in the Cold Bay accident. A lot of pilots, even airline captains, think an approach clearance is a clearance to descend to the initial approach altitude. It's not. Such a descent can be fatal. From one viewpoint, the captains of both the Cold Bay and Dulles accidents were correct. At that time, the ATC controller's manual clearly stated that the controller would protect us from terrain and obstacle conflicts by *not* issuing an approach clearance, "if terrain or traffic does not permit unrestricted descent to the lowest published altitude specified in the approach procedure prior to final descent."

That wording has since been clarified, but this is still one of those situations in which pilots will probably continue to give correct answers right out of the ATC manual and then fly their airplanes into mountains. To prevent that, we must all take the responsibility for maintaining altitude minimums back into the cockpit to protect ourselves.

We have an easy, straightforward, and fast way of accomplishing that. All we have to do is develop an MSA—Minimum Safe Altitude—awareness.

It's amazing how many of the pilots we've talked to since the Dulles crash admit they never check the MSAs before commencing an approach. The MSA should be the *first* thing they look for.

Jeppesens, which most of us have, display MSA in the upper center margin of the approach plate. Have a look at one of yours.

The bearings are inbound—that is, if the northwest quadrant is bounded by segment lines labeled 090 degrees and 180 degrees, the altitude shown in that segment is the minimum safe altitude in the enclosed area out to a distance of 25 nm from the approach facility which is named on the chart just below the MSA circle. (In the U.S., an approach facility is a VOR, NDB, or outer compass locator, not an ILS or localizer facility.) So if you are approaching the final approach aid on a heading of between 090 degrees and 180 degrees, and the sector MSA is 2500 feet, that is the lowest you should go no matter what you think ATC said. If ATC clearly tells you to go lower, confirm that he is adhering to his MVA (Minimum Vectoring Altitude).

The MSA provides at least 1000 feet of obstacle clearance within that 25 nm radius of the airport. But be aware that it's predicated on a map survey of the area. If someone erects a tall tower without the FAA's knowledge, the MSA can be in error. That's a rare occurrence but a real possibility.

The government's National Ocean Survey approach plates shows MSA with a segmented circle around the facility (with inbound bearings on the circumference) accompanied by the four MSAs in boxes inside or just outside the circle. In a number of respects, the NOS presentation is superior. It's pictorial, so you don't have to stop and draw a mental picture as you must with Jepps.

In either case, these should be the first numbers you pick off the approach plate and write on your scratch pad before beginning any approach, because in an emergency, or in event of confusion about a descent clearance, this is your minimum *safe* altitude within 25 nm of the facility prior to becoming established in the approach procedure.

You should be aware that the MSA may change from procedure to procedure to the same runway. That's because of the 25–mile arc of the sectors from the primary approach facility. As you

61

switch from an NDB to a VOR approach to an airport, the obstacles encompassed within the sectors may shift if the NDB is on the airport and the VOR is several miles away, or vice versa. (To see this difference dramatically, check the Runway 25 ILS and Runway 7 backcourse for Fort Smith, Arkansas.) It's a good idea, therefore, to glance at the MSAs for several approaches and pick the highest. Then a three or four mile error in navigation won't put you into a peak.

In that regard, incidentally, I use the highest MSA for *all* sectors shown—for two reasons. First, you can't always be certain which sector you're in. At Cold Bay, Alaska, a shift of one degree in the inbound course changes the MSA from 2800 to 10,400 feet. Second, if a facility should drop off the air or your receiver should fail, you could suddenly find yourself at a low MSA with no guidance to keep you out of an adjacent higher one.

Having developed MSA awareness, the next questions—the crucial ones—are when do you descend to the MSA and when do you descend out of it? The first is easy: Do not under any circumstances descend below the en–route MEA until you are positively within 25 nm of the approach facility.

The answer to when you can safely descend *below* the MSA is not so easy. It's *not* necessarily when the controller clears you for the approach. He can live with his errors; you can't. If he assigns an altitude lower than the sector MSA, confirm it. If for some reason you cannot get back to him, you must go back to the approach plate and search for clues.

If you have been assigned to a terminal route (depicted by a heavy arrow from a VOR, NDB, or intersection) the MEA for that route is given. (Don't confuse a terminal route with a bearing arrow on the approach plate.) But if you're being vectored or are in a non–radar environment, the safe altitude for the area may become obscure.

In view of the lack of definitive information on when to leave the MSA, then, the safest course is to *always* wait until you are established in the approach procedure as depicted on the approach plate. If that is impractical, here are a couple of rules of thumb that are *usually* safe. On a straight–in approach, stay at the MSA, or the last assigned altitude, until crossing the fix prior to the first fix shown in the descent profile. This might be an intersection or it might be the high cone in a procedure calling for a procedure turn.

After getting established on the inbound course, try to time your descent so as to maintain at least 1000 feet of altitude above the airport for each three miles from touchdown.

Back up both your own study of the approach plates and these rules of thumb with proper radio procedure. It's not required, but tell the controller what you are doing. Tell him when you leave assigned altitudes. Tell him what altitude you're descending to. If there is *any* doubt, *ask* him for a minimum altitude. It's better to seem dumb than to be dead.

A *careful* study of any approach plate will reveal ways to get down safely. The primary thing is to develop MSA awareness both for approaches and for departures. Mountains are terribly unyielding.

Squander Altitude, Die Young (March 1975)

In February of 1975, much newspaper space and newscast time were devoted to a national debate on the professionalism of pilots and air–traffic controllers. The debate was conducted by the NTSB in conjunction with their investigation of a TWA crash at Dulles on December 1, 1974.

Although we in aviation deplore seeing our dirty linen aired publicly, we can hope that the spectacle has caused a renewed and long-lasting understanding of who is responsible for keeping pilots and their passengers alive. The controllers who participated

63

in the debate made it very clear that their job is to keep pilots from bumping into one another. They *aren't* responsible for keeping us out of the trees as well.

Fair enough. Now that the air has been cleared on that point and the command responsibility has been put back in the cockpit where it belongs, let's go back to the subject of Minimum Safe Altitude Awareness and expand on it.

Obviously, there are three phases of flight during which maintaining enough altitude is crucial—departure, cruise, and approach. If there were no ATC, it's doubtful if more than one in 10,000 IFR pilots would ever have an altitude problem in either of the first two phases. ATC complicates our altitude thinking, however. For example, we once departed the Port Columbus, Ohio Airport in a 300-and-one snowstorm. The takeoff was on 28L from an intersection, while an American 727 was sitting on the departure end of 28L waiting to go. Normally we like to climb straight ahead to 1000 feet above the airport before making any turns. In order to get the 727 out as quickly as possible, however, ATC told us to turn left "after takeoff" to a heading of 230.

When is "after takeoff"? Before the Dulles debate, we would have figured the term meant after the aircraft was stabilized in a climb, which in a fixed–gear airplane is at rotation; in a retractable it would mean some time between 15 and 30 seconds after rotation. But that was assuming that ATC would not turn you toward a 1500–foot TV antenna a mile from the airport. The debate has erased all such assumptions.

Unlike the gap in communications which made it unclear who had the altitude responsibility in the Dulles fiasco (a gap which the FAA hurriedly closed with a new rule), the *Airman's Information Manual* is explicit as to who has responsibility for obstruction clearance on an IFR departure: "Each pilot, prior to departing an airport on an IFR flight, should consider the type of terrain and other obstructions on or in the vicinity of the departure airport and take the following action: (1) Determine whether a departure procedure has been established for obstruction avoidance. (2) Determine if obstruction avoidance can be maintained visually or that the departure procedure should be followed. (3) At airports where instrument approach procedures have not been established, hence no departure procedure, determine for himself what action will be necessary and take such action that will assure a safe departure."

How long has it been since you've turned your Jepp plate over to the airport diagram and checked for a departure procedure from a radar–controlled airport? Here's one that may surprise you: "IFR departure procedures: Runway 20L and 20R: Start left turn within 1 nm of airport, climb on heading of 150° to 3100' before proceeding on course." It's for DeKalb–Peachtree, Atlanta, because of an antenna off the departure end of Runway 20 that rises to 1058 feet agl.

In the absence of a published departure procedure, all the pilot can do is fall back on the minimum climb gradient criteria established by the FAA for instrument runways, and then maintain runway heading to the appropriate MSA before beginning any turns. This will slow traffic movements, but remember that the controller who asked for the turn is responsible for traffic separation; he may or may not be interested in what you need to do about obstruction avoidance. This is especially so when you are flying a light twin and want to ensure room to climb following an engine failure. Obviously, your responsibility and need must have preeminence.

En route, a problem can arise when you're approaching a higher route segment. When an MCA—Minimum Crossing Altitude—is established for the fix separating the two route segments, ATC will normally issue a climb clearance *before* the fix is reached. If there's no MCA at the fix, ATC will normally clear you for a climb immediately *after* the fix.

But don't count on it. FAR 91.119(b) makes it the pilot's responsibility to comply with MCA and MEA—Minimum En-route Altitude—limits, so he must both keep track of them and *request* a climb as appropriate.

In this regard, it's the pilot's responsibility to begin the climb early enough. For instance, if you're near Pueblo, Colorado westbound on Victor 10 at 8000 feet, flying against a high wind in a heavily loaded aircraft, don't count on ATC's starting you up soon enough to avoid hitting a rock. You'll have to request a climb in time to overcome the downdrafts over those ridges and to reach the 16,000 MEA west of Florence Intersection.

The final phase of flight, the approach, is the one that causes the greatest grief. All ATC altitude instructions in the descent must be received with skepticism. Over the last few years, ATC has grown into an omnipresent web that attempts to vector us from cradle to grave. When the trip is completed sooner than expected, however, and some pilot reaches his grave ahead of his ETA, controllers are the first to testify that responsibility and authority actually lie in the cockpit. Therefore, take command. Before descending from an altitude, *always* check to be certain you aren't being descended below the applicable MEA, MSA, or MCA. Tell the controller what you're doing, and don't be bashful about telling him what you're *not* going to do.

Our charts, although they are improved with each renewal, still do not give us as much altitude information as they should. They do not show altitude transitions, for example. Crossing altitudes at critical fixes are not shown. All of this makes it imperative that flight crews allow plenty of time to study their charts carefully and to add pertinent altitude information of their own, either to their notes or to the charts.

Finally, don't be in too big a hurry to give up altitude. Just why so many crews, particularly turbine crews, throw altitude away is the subject for a study in itself. Many of those crews and their passengers would still be alive if the old piston–pilot's motto were included on every descent checklist: "There's nothing as useless as runway behind you or altitude above you."

The Dulles Crash (March 1976)

Even after the NTSB issued its report on the TWA 727 crash at Dulles on December 1, 1974, that accident continued to be one of the most controversial mishaps in many years. The Board itself split three to two on the question of whether or not the controller erred in issuing an approach clearance when the airplane was still 44 miles from the airport with high terrain intervening.

Actually, the argument is moot. One of the piloting skills we are increasingly required to exercise is the subtle art of recognizing and correcting for errors of air traffic controllers. So we should look chiefly at what happened that December day and make sure we all thoroughly understand how to prevent similar accidents in the future.

TWA Flight 514 was inbound to Washington from Columbus, Ohio. The intended destination airport was Washington National, but en route, the crew was advised that no landings were being made at National due to high crosswinds. The captain elected to divert to Dulles.

The flight proceeded routinely toward Washington in a radar environment. It was handed off from Cleveland to Washington Center. The crew was aware early in the flight that their Dulles arrival would be a nonprecision approach to Runway 12 using the Armel VOR, which is on the airport. En route, the captain turned the flight controls over to the first officer, and the crew discussed various aspects of the Runway 12 approach. The Dulles weather was being given as 900 overcast, three to seven miles in light rain with an east wind gusting to 36 knots. There were thunderstorms in the area and a SIGMET called for moderate to severe icing in cloud.

The crew expected to fly a terminal route to the Round Hill Intersection, 17.6 miles from the airport, thence the 300–degree radial of Armel to the final approach fix, six DME northwest of the VOR. Instead, approximately 18 minutes before the crash, the crew was cleared to a heading of 090 to intercept the 300–degree radial off the Armel VOR, and to cross a point 25 nm northwest of Armel at 8000 feet. The Washington Center controller then said, " . . . the 300–degree radial will be for a VOR approach to Runway 12 at Dulles."

At the point where the flight intercepted the 300–degree radial of Armel, 84 miles out, it was several miles from the nearest designated airway or terminal route. Therefore, the crew had no way of knowing the applicable minimum altitude for the area. They had to rely totally on the controller to assign a minimum altitude until joining the terminal route at the Round Hill Intersection. Nevertheless, while the flight was still approximately 40 nm from Round Hill, it was cleared to descend to 7000 and then, at 26 nm from Round Hill, it was cleared for the approach.

The captain, judging by his remarks, expected to break out at the initial approach altitude of 1800 feet, and he was evidently anxious to do so, probably because of heavy turbulence, ice, and the possibility of penetrating a heavy storm cell. Having previously noted the only altitude shown on the chart applicable to the arrival being flown, he told his first officer, "Eighteen–hundred is the bottom."

The first officer began the descent, but three and a half minutes later the captain remarked, "You know, according to this dumb sheet, it says 3400 to Round Hill . . . is our minimum altitude."

The captain had to be reading that MEA off the terminal route depiction from Front Royal VOR to Round Hill, but there also had to be confusion about its applicability because the flight was north of that route by four or five miles.

Here, quoted directly from the NTSB report, is the discussion that followed: "The flight engineer then asked where the captain saw that and the captain replied, 'Well, here. Round Hill is eleven and a half DME.' The first officer said, 'Well, but . . . '; and the captain replied, 'When he clears you, that means you can go to your . . . ' An unidentified voice said, 'Initial approach,' and another unidentified voice said, 'Yeah!' Then the captain said, 'Initial approach altitude.' The flight engineer then said, 'We're out a . . . twenty-eight for eighteen.' An unidentified voice said, 'Right,' and someone said, 'One to go.' "

A minute and 22 seconds later the aircraft impacted on the face of Mount Weather near Berryville, Virginia.

As a result of this accident there have been several changes in ATC procedures, in approach–chart symbology, in air–carrier training procedures, and in the degree of emphasis in *Airman's Information Manual* on who is responsible for altitude awareness. Nevertheless, each pilot should personally review the unwritten rules of altitude management.

• First and foremost, the captain is responsible for maintaining adequate terrain clearance. As we have said before, a controller can live with his mistakes; a pilot can't. This has been proven in at least four tragic accidents over the past few years. As a consequence, the pilot should always double check the controller when it comes to altitude assignments, whether the assignments are actual or implied. When you are vectored off a published route, *always* check to make certain the altitude assignment is safe for the area into which you are being vectored. When you are cleared to descend, *never* assume the controller knows something you don't; if the altitude given or implied is lower than MEAs in the locality, make the controller convince you it's safe to descend.

• Always give the controller a chance to change his mind.

CAUSE AND CIRCUMSTANCE

Among careful pilots the practice is to tell the controller what altitude is being left and what altitude is being descended to. Had the captain of Flight 514 told the Dulles approach controller he was leaving 7000 for 1800, the accident might have been prevented.

• Don't be in a hurry to get down. When the ceiling is broken, moderately low, and visibility is good underneath, as was true that day at Dulles, the urge is to drop on down and get visual contact with the ground. That urge must be ignored. Try to stay about 1000 feet above the airport for each three miles to touchdown.

• Be aware of the MSA. Most (but not all) approach plates have Minimum Safe Altitude information depicted on them. This should be the first altitude you look for on the chart when preparing for an approach. You should descend below the MSA for the sector you're in with the greatest reluctance and only when you're certain that it's safe to do so.

En route (when more than 25 nm from the approach facility, which is the outer limit of the MSA) we study the MEAs for the area carefully whenever we are vectored off designated airways. This is not an infallible precaution, of course, because a mountain peak may stick up between a pair of airways far above either MEA, but it's a clue.

If off airways, we try to maintain at least 2000 feet above the highest MEA for the area.

Another Case of Premature Descent? (May 1976)

The NTSB's report on the crash of a Wolfe Industries King Air during approach to Washington National Airport on January 25, 1975 is worth studying by every pilot. The aircraft struck a 765–foot (msl) antenna while conducting a VOR/DME approach to Runway 18. The Board split on the probable cause along the same

70

lines as it did for the TWA crash at Dulles a month earlier, and for the same reasons.

The majority determined that "the probable cause of this accident was an unauthorized descent below the published minimum approach segment altitude . . . for reasons undetermined."

The dissenting members, Francis McAdams and Isabel Burgess, wrote, "Although we agree that the unauthorized descent was a cause of the accident, we believe that the failure of ATC to either defer the clearance, issue altitude restrictions or issue a timely safety advisory was also a cause of the accident."

As was true of the Board's finding in the case of the TWA crash at Dulles, neither the majority nor the minority really advanced aviation safety with their determinations in this instance. Certainly the crew of the King Air should have adhered to the charted descents in the VOR/DME approach, and certainly the controllers —if they did indeed see that the aircraft was too low—should have issued an urgent advisory. The evidence is they were discussing the altitude at least 20 seconds before impact. But in substance, that is saying the airplane crashed because it ran out of altitude.

What might have caused the captain of this King Air to descend prematurely is the critical issue. The report on the accident gives us few clues; however, with a bit of reading between the lines, two possibilities come to mind. First let's look at what happened.

The King Air was inbound to Washington National from Columbus, Ohio. The flight was routine to a point about 30 northwest of DCA. At 1158:20 the copilot checked in with Washington, level at 8000. The copilot was working the radios, and presumably the captain was flying. Approach cleared the aircraft down to 5000 feet at 1204:20, and then for the Runway 18 VOR/DME approach at 1204:51. The flight was south (to the right) of the inbound radial (153 degrees) and 18 miles from the airport at that instant.

The weather was 700 overcast, visibility 20 miles with a strong right–to–left crosswind aloft relative to the approach course.

71

CAUSE AND CIRCUMSTANCE

The reconstructed radar trace shows that the aircraft flew a course of about 145 degrees, crossed through the 153–degree radial until it was a mile off course to the left and then began to correct slowly back towards the centerline. The reconstructed encoding altimeter plot shows that it descended in a more or less straight line down to approximately 720 feet and struck the tower at about 1210:00. It was five miles from DCA, a half–mile off centerline and about 780 feet below the altitude called for on the approach profile for the five–nm DME fix when it hit.

The only clue in the NTSB's report that might explain the descent to below the depicted profile was an erroneous altimeter setting given to another aircraft on the frequency about a minute after the King Air reported in to the DCA final approach controller. The correct altimeter setting was 29.41. At about 1205:30, Piedmont 910 asked for the latest altimeter and the final approach controller answered, "Ah, three zero four one." The Piedmont crew later testified they heard only the " . . . four one" and so didn't change their setting. The NTSB considered the possibility that the King Air crew had heard the erroneous setting and had reset their altimeters to it, but dismissed that as a probable cause. The captain's altimeter, a counter–drum–pointer type, was recovered. It was set at 29.40.

The copilot's altimeter was not recovered. The Board considered the possibility that only the copilot's altimeter was reset to the erroneous 30.41, and that *it* was used for altitude reference. The investigators decided that such a thing was highly unlikely, because the captain, who was presumably flying, would then have had to look across to the right side of the panel for altitude information.

We cannot afford to jump to that conclusion so quickly, however. The winds that day were southwest and increasing from 10 knots on the surface to 37 knots at only 4000 feet. It was probably bumpy (the accident report doesn't say) and since the barometric

72

pressure was unnaturally low, the copilot (28 years old and 1963 total hours) may not have thought it unusual for the pressure to change one inch over the period of 10 or 15 minutes since they'd last heard ATIS.

If we accept that premise, we see that the crew would have been faced with several potential altitude awareness errors. For example, perhaps the captain, busy with both turbulence and an off–course situation due to the heavy crosswind, was relying on the copilot to call altitude. He may have simply cross–checked the pointer on his altimeter and not the readout on the drum.

A little far–fetched, but it reminds us that the possibility of altimeter–setting errors should be considered in all two–pilot operations. A checklist requirement that at least one crewman ensure correspondence between all altimeters before descent below the MSA is excellent insurance.

A second possible cause for this accident, which the NTSB did not address because it is purely speculative, might have been the 20–mile visibility on the surface. We have all experienced that potential killer. The air is rough, a strong crosswind has sent us through the final approach course and occasional breaks in the overcast reveal excellent VFR conditions just a couple of hundred feet lower. When that occurs, the urge to push on down and pick up visual references sometimes is overpowering.

We cannot suggest that this crew succumbed to that temptation, but the evidence, especially the altitude plot, suggests it *could* have been the cause. That should remind us that pilots must be resolute—we *must* adhere to all altitude restrictions until the airport or runway environment is solidly in view.

There is one final lesson to be learned from this accident: Some approaches require more altitude awareness than others. Although you can be casual about holding to the final approach course and staying on altitude to runways like Oklahoma City's

73

35 or Jacksonville's 7, others do not allow errors of such magnitude.

The VOR/DME Runway 18 approach at DCA has the smallest allowance for error of any approach we've experienced. Within a couple of miles of that course there are two antennas which reach above 1000 feet msl, two others which go above 700 feet, and several which are above 400 feet. Before shooting this approach, or any approach for that matter, the pilot should take a red grease pencil and mark each obstruction shown on the plate to be within a 10-mile radius of the airport, that will be sticking up into the clouds when the ceiling is at minimums.

That's an almost certain cure for any tendency to descend prematurely, whatever the cause.

TOUCHDOWN 6

Everyone measures the quality of a pilot on his execution of the touchdown, so we all try especially hard to make each one perfect. Why, then, is the poor touchdown a leading cause of accidents?

The Three Faces of Landing Accidents (June 1974)

With virtually no fear of later being proven wrong, one can forecast that next month 70 business aircraft, ranging from Cessna 182s up through G–IIs, will be substantially damaged by overshoots, undershoots or outright loss of control in the flare, touchdown, or rollout.

Our poor landing record has safety people totally perplexed. The landing is used by most pilots (and their passengers as well) as the yardstick of their flying skills, so you'd think we would all concentrate hard on making the touchdown perfect, and thus keep it at the bottom of the accident–cause list.

Not so. For businessmen pilots, the final 30 seconds of the flight accounts for about 20 percent of their accidents; the larger the aircraft, the higher the percentage. For corporate turbine crews, the final 30 seconds accounts for a whopping 58 percent of the bent airplanes.

You don't have to search through accident statistics very long

75

before you realize that those percentages are slightly misleading. Small–airplane pilots aren't less susceptible to the landing mishap; they're just lucky in having long runways to land on 90 percent of the time. Discounting groundloops in little airplanes, the occasional showoff ("Watch me make the first turnoff!") and hydroplaning incidents, virtually all landing accidents are the result of trying to get into an airport that is too short for either the airplane or the pilot's skill.

Enough has already been written about the minimum runway requirement: The pilot who doesn't know by now that he needs at least two–thirds more runway than the aircraft flight manual shows is probably beyond help. Let's look, instead, at some of the other landing traps we fall into.

One trap is that of placing too much reliance on past experience rather than on an analysis of current conditions. If we would all just check the charts in the aircraft manual and add two–thirds to the distance shown before each landing, we'd probably eliminate a dozen or so of those 70 accidents that occur each month.

That practice would make us stop and think. One of my most horrifying moments in an airplane came just after touching down on a little strip I'd been into a hundred times before without incident. I tapped the brakes and discovered that early morning dew had made the grass slippery as glass. I just hadn't thought.

Heavy-airplane pilots seldom have that particular problem, but here's something that does often occur: The boss says he wants to stop off at Chitlin Corners, Iowa on the way home. Without hesitation, our hero, who remembers stopping there a half–dozen times last year, readily agrees.

Two hours later he's sitting 600 feet beyond the upwind end of Chitlin Corners International's only runway looking a corn worm in the eye and wondering what happened.

For starters, he forgot that last year all the stops at CCI had been on a westbound leg from home base with only 1500 pounds of fuel remaining. Today he came from Denver and therefore touched down with 2500 pounds. That extra 1000 pounds added six percent to the stopping distance. Also, a year ago all the arrivals had been in the early morning. The warmest he saw was +5°C. Today it was mid–afternoon and +15. Add another four percent. Finally, a year ago all landings were to the northwest over the corn patch he's now in. Today he landed to the southeast and there's a 15–foot tree on that opposite approach. Add another 10 percent. In addition, the runway had a one percent gradient—for a net two percent downgrade change from previous landings on the runway and another seven percent on the length requirement. The 4500–foot runway that was comfortable last year was precisely 600 feet short today—by the book.

A second landing problem is a misunderstanding about the flare and touchdown profile. The famous last words are: "It's a short runway so let's touch down right on the end."

If you've got to touch down on the very end to stop before skidding into a daisy patch, the runway isn't legal. Landing field length charts assume the aircraft will cross the threshold at an altitude of 50 feet. Wise pilots do just that.

If you must make a choice—touch down on the very end or risk skidding off the other end—it's far better to run off the other end at 30 knots than to hit the lip of the runway threshold at 130 knots. Undershoots account for approximately 30 percent of landing accidents. If we would all determine to eliminate them by crossing the threshold at no less than the specified height, the worst possible outcome would be a transfer of about 250 accidents a year from landed–short to the overrun category. Even that would result in a net improvement in our safety record, because significantly fewer fatalities occur in overruns than in undershoots, and the damage to aircraft is less.

The third type of landing accident is loss of control. In the case of small aircraft, some of these are on long runways and are due to a lack of skill in handling a crosswind, wheelbarrowing and/or a failure to initiate a go–around until too late.

The only way we can eliminate those accidents is to emphasize the basics in initial and recurrency training for businessmen. It's a hotly debated point, but my own feeling is that most of these accident causes would be cured if little–airplane pilots would simply hold the nosewheel up longer in the rollout. I've seen airplanes as big as a DC–6 wheelbarrow out of control when the pilot shoved forward on the yoke instantly after touchdown.

Loss of control isn't limited to unskilled, little–airplane pilots. From 25 to 30 percent of the landing accidents in corporate jets flown by professional crews are attributable to loss of control. Most of them result from stalls or from impacting the runway at a high sink rate while attempting to squeeze the airplane into an airport that is too short.

The frequency of these accidents is causing some aviation safety experts to take a jaundiced look at the traditional 1.3 V_{SO} approach speed. The problem is not 1.3 V_{SO}, but how V_{SO} is determined. The manufacturer has a vested interest in making it as low as possible, so he sometimes installs flow strips, twists the wings, adds leading edge cuffs and whatnot to delay the stall until the aircraft is as far back as possible on the drag curve and in a high sink when V_{SO} arrives. On my own airplane, 1.3 V_{SO} is much too slow. Experimentation has shown that with forward CG loading, there's not quite enough elevator or lift left to flare properly or pick up a high sink due to a last second wind shear. You should experiment with your aircraft, and if the margin is too slim, adjust your approach speed accordingly. Having done that, you'll also have to adjust the landing distances shown in the charts. A good rule of thumb is to increase the runway requirement 100 feet for each one knot increase in approach speed above the book figure —then divide the result by 0.6 to find the actual, *safe* length needed.

TOUCHDOWN

In the final analysis, landing accidents will be decreased by a combination of more realistic landing data in flight manuals, better training, and improved procedures.

Whatever effort it takes, the result can be a dramatic improvement in business aviation's safety record.

Touchdown Accidents (July 1975)

It is well known that the approach/landing accident accounts for 58 percent of the total number of accidents in business jets. That's far too many, but it makes the task of improving our record easy —we just need to concentrate our safety efforts on the last 30 seconds of each flight.

With that in mind, let's look at two approach/landing accidents in the NTSB records and see what went wrong. The root causes are clear: wind shear and pride.

Wind Shear——On November 27, 1973, a Delta DC–9 struck approach lights at Chattanooga, Tennessee and slid to a stop on the runway. There were no fatalities, but the aircraft was destroyed.

This was a classic wind shear accident, compounded by optical refraction through a rain–covered windshield and a glideslope signal that brought the aircraft across the middle marker at the lower limit.

The approach was shot into a thunderstorm with 400 scattered to broken clouds and two miles visibility. The crew conducted an exemplary coupled ILS approach to the decision height—with one important oversight. Neither pilot noticed that the rate of sink and airspeed were increasing in the final few seconds before DH, or that the nose was being trimmed down by the autopilot.

The NTSB's calculations of the wind shear on the approach show the headwind decreasing from 32 knots at the outer marker to five knots on the surface—a difference of 27 knots. In that

79

situation, an ILS approach will begin at a low groundspeed and rate of sink, both of which will increase rapidly as the descent progresses along the glideslope. Therefore, in a decreasing headwind situation during a coupled approach, the autopilot will trim the airplane's nose down to stay on the glideslope. Thus, when the autopilot is uncoupled, the pilot will take command of an airplane that is in the wrong attitude for the flare and grossly out of trim. Add heavy rain, which can make the threshold appear lower and farther away than it actually is, and it's very likely that some approach lights will be clipped. To prevent that, put the following in your mental checklist:

• When approaching in a thunderstorm, *always* ask *both* approach control and the tower if there have been any reports of wind shear. Only six minutes before this accident, a Learjet had shot the approach with some difficulty and, after landing, had reported a wind shear condition to the tower. Evidently that information was not passed on to the DC–9 crew, nor did the crew ask for it.

• When wind shear is a possibility, try to capture the glideslope a little farther out, then watch the attitude, power requirement and rate of sink carefully. If, at a constant airspeed, on glideslope, they change perceptibly, you're in a wind shear situation and you can expect a critical transition from the instrument to visual segment of the approach, as well as a critical flare. The sink rate of the Chattanooga DC–9 increased from 462 feet in the vicinity of the outer marker to 1050 feet near the middle marker. Yet after the accident, the crew reported that the approach was stabilized. It obviously was not.

• In a wind shear situation, be cocked and primed for a go-around if the approach begins to come unglued in the final seconds —even if (perhaps *especially* if) the approach is visual. In this instance the approach was visual for a minute and 37 seconds. Three seconds after calling the middle marker, the copilot called out, "Gotta plus five (bug speed plus five), sinking to nine (900 fpm descent)," and 6.5 seconds later, "Plus five, sinking to 10."

The sink rate was obviously worsening for some reason, and had the pilot initiated a go–around at that instant he would have had 100 feet of altitude above the touchdown zone to transition into a climb. Instead, he continued the approach because it *looked* right.

A split second before the aircraft hit the first light stanchion, the visual clues to an excessive sink rate suddenly came into focus, but it was too late.

Pride——At 2221 hours on October 28, 1973, a Piedmont 737 ran off the end of Runway 14 at Greensboro, North Carolina. There were no fatalities, but the aircraft was substantially damaged.

This was another thunderstorm–related accident. The weather was 400 scattered, 1500 overcast, one mile in very heavy rain. The wind was from 320 at eight. Greensboro had two instrument runways at that time: A front course ILS served Runway 14, which is 6380 feet long, and a VOR/DME procedure served Runway 23, which is 8201 feet long. Seven minutes before the accident, another captain had elected to shoot the VOR/DME approach to Runway 23, which was more into the wind and 1821 feet longer; he had experienced no difficulty. The captain of the 737 elected to shoot the ILS to the shorter, downwind runway.

The approach lights were acquired shortly after crossing the outer marker, and the captain hand flew the airplane to touchdown using visual references. There is no VASI on Runway 14, but halfway in from the outer marker both pilots noted that the airplane was high—about half full–scale on the indicator bar, according to the copilot.

Just before flare, the copilot called out, "Plus eight, down eight," meaning bug speed plus eight knots and sinking 800 fpm. The touchdown was right wheels, then, 300 feet later, the nosewheel, and finally the left wheels 400 feet after the right ones. When all three gears had finally contacted the surface, only 3380 feet of wet runway remained. The aircraft hydroplaned off the end, crossed a service road, lost all three gears, and came to rest 820 feet beyond the runway.

This accident obviously calls for more notes in your mental checklist:

• When inbound to a wet airport, stack all the odds in your favor. Piedmont's Boeing 737 manual states that 5000 feet are required to land on a wet runway using brakes, spoilers, and reverse, and the Jepp chart for Greensboro cautions that only 5030 feet are available beyond the glideslope touchdown point. Considering that he had an eight–knot tailwind as well, this captain left himself *no* margin. (Without reverse, the 737 needs 7600 feet to land on a wet runway, so the captain was betting everything on the reversers working.) In addition, Runway 14 at Greensboro slopes down 26 feet in the first 3350 feet, making it difficult to get onto it short, even in the best of conditions.

• Again, be ready to go around, and don't be too proud to do so. This approach was never stabilized, and the middle marker was crossed high and hot. One doesn't like to shoot an approach into a thunderstorm, find the airport, then chuck it all to go out and punch into the cell again, but the possibility of a missed approach must be a major part of the decision to begin an approach in the first place. It would seem fundamental that you never fly into anything you are unwilling to fly out of.

Although both of these accidents occurred to air carrier aircraft, there's not that much difference between a DC–9 and a G–II, or between a DC–9 and a light twin, for that matter. If during every approach we'd all pay closer attention to wind shear and procedures—and curb pride—we could rather easily decrease our overall accident rate 30 to 40 percent.

The Touchdown-Then-Go Accident (July 1977)

Within the space of 22 days last year, two accidents occurred when captains landed long, tried to stop, changed their minds, tried to go, changed their minds again, and finally tried—much too late—to stop.

Those two accidents, both in Boeing 727s, one in Alaska and the other at St. Thomas, Virgin Islands, point to a problem that has troubled every pilot of heavy equipment at some time in his career: After touching down on a runway, how much time have you got in which to change your mind and take off again?

The answer to that question is difficult, so let's look at these two accidents for possible clues.

The first occurred on April 5, 1976 at Ketchikan, Alaska. The reported weather at the time was ceiling 800 feet obscured, visibility 1.5 miles in light snow and fog. The temperature was +2°C.

The actual weather, however, was evidently much better than reported. The crew told investigators they had acquired ground contact at 4000 feet in the descent and had picked up the approach lights at two miles. The captain conducted a visual approach to Runway 11, which is 7497 feet long, plus a 100–foot stopway. Braking action was reported as poor.

According to the NTSB report, the approach was not well executed. The altitude trace shows that the airplane was significantly below the glideslope until it was 3.5 miles from the runway threshold. More important, the airspeed was very high throughout the approach. At about 2.25 miles from touchdown the airspeed was still 210 knots, and the touchdown was at 145 knots.

From that sort of approach, it's not surprising that the touchdown was about 3300 feet down the runway. The captain, who was flying, deployed the ground spoilers, reversed the engines and applied the brakes. When he discovered that the braking action was indeed poor, he retracted the spoilers, called for

25 degrees flaps, and advanced the throttles for takeoff thrust.

For some reason, the reversers did not stow, and so forward thrust could not be obtained. The captain tried to get the reversers to stow by applying a burst of reverse and then placing the throttles at idle. That didn't work, so he pulled back into full reverse, again deployed the spoilers and raised the nose as the aircraft crossed the end of the runway. The 727 came to rest 700 feet beyond the far end of the stopway.

Just 22 days later, at St. Thomas, an almost identical accident occurred. In this instance, the weather was 2500 scattered and 25 miles visibility. Jet landings at the Harry S. Truman Airport are on Runway 9, which is 4658 feet long, plus a 500–foot overrun. The wind was given as 120 degrees at 12 knots.

In this instance, the captain flew a normal approach, utilizing the ILS, at $V_{REF} + 10$. He was using 30 degrees of flaps, although somewhat ambiguous company rules called for 40 degrees for the reported wind.

The aircraft crossed the threshold at a normal elevation and seemed destined for a touchdown on the aiming point 1000 feet down the runway. But then turbulence was encountered, and the right wing dropped alarmingly. The captain held the aircraft off and rolled in almost full aileron to level the aircraft. These actions set up a float, and finally the captain jammed the airplane onto the runway about 2800 feet beyond the threshold.

He immediately decided to go around and moved the throttles to the straight–up position—the 1.4 EPR position—and waited for the power to come up so he could advance the throttles to full power.

The EPR still didn't come up, so the captain pushed the throttles to the stops. When the EPR didn't rise as quickly as expected, he closed the throttles and began braking hard. The aircraft skidded up over a small hill and came to rest 525 feet beyond the end of the overrun area.

Based on these two accidents, the conclusion must be that a go–around should not be attempted once the aircraft has touched down, certainly not after an attempt is made to stop. But that conclusion is at odds with experience. Heavy aircraft have often been landed and then flown out into a go–around with total success.

So, a go–around following a landing and attempted stop *can* be done. The question is, what can be learned from these two accidents that will tell us when it *can't* be done?

For the Alaskan crash, the answer is obvious. A successful touchdown–then–go must be preplanned. Apparently this captain had not done so.

A successful touchdown–then–go from a fast approach must be flawlessly executed. Simple mathematical computation reveals the reason for that. At a touchdown speed of 145 knots, about 245 feet of runway zips by each second. If 10 seconds are allowed for touching down, testing the braking action and initiating the go–around—plus another seven seconds for the engines to spool up—the very minimum runway requirement is 6000 feet. This allows for a touchdown 1000 feet beyond the threshold, plus another 800 feet at the far end for climb to the obstacle height.

If the reversers are deployed, approximately 1500 additional feet are needed for the deploy and stow cycles. Totaling it all up, the runway length needed is 7500 feet, which is every inch this captain had—*if* he'd touched down at the 1000–foot mark. As it happened, he touched down at about the 3300–foot mark.

At St. Thomas, the captain had to deal with the same mathematics, except that all the numbers were smaller. Following this accident, Boeing conducted a touch–and–go investigation for the NTSB and discovered that about 1900 feet of runway, plus 800 feet for climb, are needed to go around in the 727 if the procedure is initiated at 120 knots. The total, then, is 2400 feet. But since he touched down 2800 feet beyond the threshold on a 5158–foot runway, including the overrun, this captain had only 2358 feet in which to complete a maneuver requiring 2400 feet.

Now, back to that original question: How long have you got to initiate a go-around after touchdown? When the question is phrased like that, there is no answer. As these two captains learned, it depends on where you touched down. The question should be: How long have you got to initiate a go-around after crossing the threshold? Too few pilots have troubled to find an answer to that.

For most business aircraft the answer is very simple. Each second after crossing the threshold the remaining runway diminishes by about 200 feet. Since you'll need a minimum of 2500 feet remaining to go around, subtract 2500 from the runway length and divide the answer by 200. On a 5500–foot runway, notice, the result is 15; for a 6000–foot runway it's 17, and so on. So when you cross the threshold, start counting, "one–thousand–one, one–thousand–two, one–thousand–three . . . "

Out there around one–thousand–fifteen, time will have run out. Don't attempt a go–around after that magic number has been counted off.

Must Bad Winds Equal Bad Landings? (December 1976)

Landing accidents due to wind routinely fall into three broad categories: Landing short or hard, losing control after touchdown, overrunning the runway. Let's have a look at each.

Wind shear normally gets the blame for short or hard landings, and quite often a wind shear is indeed involved. But millions of landings have been successfully negotiated in shifty wind conditions, so that's rarely a genuine excuse for plopping in short or banging down hard enough to fold a gear.

The universally accepted technique for overcoming wind shear and/or heavy gusts, of course, is more airspeed. The general rule of thumb is add one–half the gust factor to the normal approach speed. At controlled airports, where the gust factor is reported, that is easily done.

The problem is quite different at uncontrolled airports, however. Before the rule of thumb can be applied, the pilot first must determine if wind shear or significant gusts exist and what their magnitude is. The windsock is a tremendous aid, but when it's on or near buildings, every little bit of wind whipping around corners will cause it to indicate gusts, when, in fact, the wind in the touchdown zone may be tame.

So the windsock must be cross–checked against other clues. Wind patterns on water are best. You will also see wind patterns in grain fields or even in fields of tall grass. Trees can give a clue as well, but they're hard to "read."

If wind patterns cannot be seen, the pilot must resort to educated guesses. When there's a strong wind on the surface and the airport is surrounded by rough or hilly terrain, trees, or buildings, he can be assured he'll encounter mechanical turbulence, or shear, as he approaches the touchdown zone. The wise pilot always studies the lay of the land relative to the wind as much as time allows during the approach to landing. He also looks for wind patterns on every landing. After a while, gauging the magnitude of turbulence becomes a subconscious thing, and the pilot adds appropriate speed.

This, of course, only scratches the surface of the windy–day, landed–short/landed–hard problem. But we believe that most of these accidents can be avoided if the pilot will just learn to judge the wind and *anticipate* the magnitude of the gust or shear.

One final note. In most business aircraft and at most airports they're flown into, as we've said,. it's not necessary to touch down within the first 50 feet of the runway. Trying to land short on windy days—on a runway five times the length needed—has led to more serious accidents than any other error in judgment.

87

Loss–of–control after touchdown on a windy day almost never occurs to a *turbine* pilot on a dry runway, according to NTSB records. For the turbine pilot, the set–up for running off the side of the runway into a ditch or snowbank is a heavy crosswind and a slick runway. In that situation, nosewheel steering will be relatively ineffective, braking will be poor to none and both will be aggravated by unfavorable force vectors when reverse thrust is applied. Picture an aircraft sliding along a runway slightly weathercocked into the wind with reverse thrust applied. That is what is meant by unfavorable thrust vectors.

For the *piston* pilot, loss of control on the rollout is almost always a manifestation of poor training. What usually happens is that the pilot touches down flat, perhaps even nosewheel first, then he jams the control wheel forward in an effort to paste the airplane onto the runway. When he does that, the combination of high speed, effective flaps, and lots of lift at the elevator will raise the main gear off the ground, after which nosewheel steering becomes totally ineffective. Aircraft with stabilators are the very worst on this score.

Prevention is relatively simple. The touchdown should be a wee bit hot, but the aircraft must be flared enough to result in the nosewheel's coming down *after* the mains. This ensures that some lift will be dumped at touchdown.

In a light aircraft, it's important that after touchdown the elevators be lowered only enough—through a slight relaxation of backpressure—to ensure positive nosewheel contact. That slight adjustment results in effective nosewheel steering and maximum weight on the mains to prevent lateral skidding and to provide good braking. Normally, once the brakes are applied, the control wheel can be pulled all the way back to throw even greater weight onto the mains.

Finally, there's the matter of using the ailerons properly during rollout in a bad crosswind. The natural tendency is to apply them exactly backward. Think about it. If the airplane is tending to weathercock to the left because of a left gust, the poorly trained pilot will impulsively fall back on automobile–driving instincts and try to steer out of it by rolling the wheel right. This results in the left aileron's going down, which increases lift—and therefore drag—on the upwind side. Instead of being counteracted, the weathercocking tendency is abetted. The preventative is obvious and automatic to wind–wise pilots. Immediately upon touchdown, the ailerons should go full into the wind and stay there.

With the overrun accident, the tendency is to point back to the preventative for the undershoot and hard–landing problem—that is, a high approach and touchdown speed—and say you can't win, which isn't true. Studies of overrun accidents seldom disclose one that was solely due to carrying extra speed over the threshold so as to protect against wind–gradient effects or wind shear.

The predominant cause of overshoots is landing *downwind*. It's remarkable how many experienced pilots forget to check the wind direction before landing. It's absolutely astounding how many continue to try to get onto the runway and stop long after it should have become screamingly evident that they *were* landing downwind.

This type of accident has to be the result of complacency mixed with large doses of pride. The preventative measure for the over-run accident when wind is a factor is simply a resolve to go around and try it again if the first attempt doesn't work out. Of course you must carry extra speed over the threshold to avoid the under-shoot or hard landing. But if the airplane begins to float—perhaps because you arrived in the touchdown zone concurrently with a lull between gusts—go around and hope that Dame Fortune smiles on your next try.

One final note: Remember that it's far, far better to err and carry too much extra speed in the approach and consequently run off the far end of the runway than to err on the too–slow side. The record is very clear; far more fatalities occur in undershoots and hard landings than in overshoots.

Much, much more needs to be said about the windy–day landing accident. But more important is that we all need to apply what we *already* know.

ATTITUDES ON THE FLIGHT DECK

7

Human error is frequently cited as a cause of accidents, but that's no help. To err is human, and only God can change that. Attitudes, however, are another matter.

Is the Captain Always Right? (June 1977)

The worst aviation disaster in history—the collision of two 747s on the ground in the Canary Islands last winter—will no doubt be discussed and speculated about for years to come. *Why* did *either* captain agree to taxi the length of the active runway in such poor visibility? *Why* didn't the Pan Am captain wait until the KLM 747 had departed before going onto the active? *Why* did the KLM captain begin his takeoff before he was certain that the other aircraft was clear?

And then there is the *prime* question for all crewmembers everywhere: How could all six of the highly qualified aviators involved, three on each flight deck, have been listening to the several conversations with ATC and still fail to realize that an extremely dangerous situation was developing?

An interesting bit of side speculation on that is the possibility that one crewman did become nervous but didn't speak out or was overridden by his captain. In the case of this particular accident, that's only speculation, but in numerous other instances, crashes have occurred despite the fact that some crewmember expressed his uneasiness about a potential problem.

The classic instance was the infamous New Haven, Connecticut crash. On approach to the beach–side airport, the first officer told his captain they weren't more than 20 feet off the water. He was ignored and the aircraft slammed into a beach house.

In 1973, as the result of that Connecticut crash, the NTSB raised a question about what the second–in–command should do when he becomes convinced his captain is in error. The apparently obvious answer—take command—is totally unacceptable. Certainly there are situations in which the copilot should take command, but guidelines are impossible to delineate, except in instances of obvious incapacitation. Were the judgment of when to take over left to the second–in–command, accidents would undoubtedly increase.

The reasons why the captain's authority must not be questioned in the air are clear. He is usually the most experienced man in the cockpit, so the odds are that his decisions will be correct if there's a difference of opinion. It's always better to go with the odds.

That is well and good, but it leaves a wide gap through which accidents can occur in spite of someone in the cockpit having a better idea.

That is an extremely difficult problem to resolve. Flight is a very dynamic situation. Sometimes the second–in–command hesitates even to question his captain, and rightfully so, because there's usually no time for the commander to reevaluate his decisions and modify his actions. Certainly, there's seldom time for the second–in–command to conduct a meaningful analysis of the captain's actions, perhaps confer with another crewmember or occupant of the aircraft, and then elect to take over.

There is, however, a partial solution that might have prevented a rather large number of accidents. If captains would work just a little harder at creating the right atmosphere and spirit in the cockpit there could, and would, be an easy flow of information that would in no way dilute the captain's authority but would occasionally alert him to his own errors.

That spirit must begin with the attitude—and indeed the very personality—of the captain himself. An effective aircraft commander must be one of those relatively rare individuals who can be decisive, but never cocksure. Vacillation has no place in the left front seat of an aircraft, but neither does totalitarianism. A captain must be sure of himself, but never too proud to reevaluate a decision that's been questioned or to accept advice.

Actions that extend all the way back to the home office may affect a captain's ability to do that. Company management—the captain's boss or bosses—must never do or say anything that could make a captain feel unsure of himself. If he sits in the left seat uncertain just how tight his seat belt is cinched down—how secure his job is—it's much more difficult for him to accept the advice of subordinates gracefully.

Assuming that there is no question about his authority, the captain should feel free to encourage a beneficial flow of *operational* conversation in the cockpit. He doesn't *have* to act on any of it, but he shouldn't resent it either. If he's 10 knots off the bug speed and knows it—perhaps he is keeping the speed high because his intuition tells him to expect a wind shear at the middle marker —he should see no harm in the copilot's mentioning it. After they're on the ground the captain can even use the incident as a takeoff point for a discussion of wind shear techniques.

The same is true for traffic call–outs. We've ridden with captains who seemed to resent having traffic they'd already spotted being pointed out to them. That's ridiculous, of course, because how is the subordinate supposed to know the danger has

93

been spotted if the captain has remained silent?

To encourage comments, remarks and advice from other crew-members, the captain should acknowledge each one. We once flew extensively with a man who responded with a code that even he probably wasn't aware he was using. When someone would mention that he was low on the glideslope and he hadn't noticed, he would say "Thanks" and begin to pick it up. If he'd seen it earlier and was either already correcting or had a reason for not correcting, he would simply say "Roger." Thus we knew from his response what to expect. "Thanks" meant he would correct whatever had been called out; "Roger" meant he was aware of the situation but would not correct for reasons he'd give later.

One day he didn't respond with "thanks" or "Roger" to a traffic call–out, and everyone on the flight deck knew instantly that he hadn't heard it.

Subordinates also have a role in creating an open atmosphere on the flight deck. The object in giving advice is that it be heeded. But the manner in which some junior crewmen give it makes it almost humanly impossible for the captain to respond. We once knew a first officer who preceded every comment with, "If I were you, I'd . . . ." His advice was seldom taken even when it should have been.

Normally it's enough simply to give a value or state a fact. "Outer marker with the gear to go" is much more tactful than "You forgot the gear, I'll put it down for you." "Bug speed plus 10" is better than "You're 10 knots fast, better slow it up." A subordinate who editorializes is going to be invited to shut up, probably to the detriment of safety.

The proper relationship and atmosphere on the flight deck should be fundamental, but that's too often not the case. To create it, the captain must first be able to admit that he might be wrong, and other crewmembers must recognize that, right or wrong, he's the boss.

That's all contrary to human nature, but in this instance, going against human nature is both necessary and worthwhile.

Cockpit Discipline (September 1975)

Normally in writing on aviation safety we analyze NTSB reports rather than parrot them. The reason for this is the constraint under which NTSB investigators must work. The Safety Board is a fact–gathering body, so it cannot dwell on suppositions, no matter how obvious they may be, or elaborate on the human problems that lie behind virtually every accident. Analysis of that sort must be left to a responsible and concerned press, and we ordinarily endeavor to fulfill that obligation.

But once in a while, an NTSB report comes down that needs no analysis. The initial release on the cause of a crash of a scheduled DC–9 at Charlotte, North Carolina in September 1974 is a case in point. There is a possibility that a misreading of the altimeters was a contributing cause of this accident, but in their release the Board elaborated at length on *why* the altimeters—as well as other indications of an impending crash—may have been misread.

Here are pertinent quotes from the NTSB release:

> As the result of its investigation of this accident, the Safety Board determined that the probable cause of the Charlotte crash was the flightcrew's lack of altitude awareness at critical points during the approach due to poor cockpit discipline in that the crew did not follow prescribed procedures.
>
> The DC–9, operating as Eastern Flight 212, was on a scheduled passenger flight from Charleston, South Carolina to Chicago, Illinois with an enroute stop at Charlotte. The flight departed Charleston at 0700 and was cleared to Charlotte on an instrument flight plan. The first officer was flying the aircraft while the captain handled all radio transmissions and checklist items.

CAUSE AND CIRCUMSTANCE

At 0724, the Airport Terminal Information Service broadcast the Charlotte weather, which was received by Flight 212, as sky partially obscured; estimated ceiling 4000 broken, 12,000 broken; visibility 1½ in ground fog . . . wind 360 degrees at five . . . VOR 36 approach in use . . . .

During the 34–minute flight from Charleston, numerous radio contacts were maintained by Flight 212 with the Federal Aviation Administration's Atlanta air route traffic control center and subsequently with the Charlotte approach and local controller. At 0725:05 Atlanta cleared the flight to contact Charlotte, and 13 seconds later Charlotte approach control provided vectors to the final approach course for Runway 36. At 0731:09 the final controller cleared the flight for a VOR 36 approach and stated, "You're six miles south of Ross Intersection."

Ross Intersection is the final approach fix point for Runway 36 at Charlotte. At 0732:01 the captain told the first officer that the upcoming fix point was "Ross, five point five, eighteen hundred." This information indicated Ross was located 5.5 nautical miles from the VOR facility on the airport with a minimum crossing altitude of 1800 feet mean sea level. At 0733:17 the captain said, "There's Ross. Now we can go down." At 0733:36 the captain advised the Charlotte Tower that they were by Ross Intersection and the local controller cleared the flight to land on Runway 36. Twenty–two seconds later, the DC–9 hit trees, then struck the ground and broke up and burned 1.7 miles from the Ross Intersection.

According to the cockpit voice recorder, the flightcrew engaged intermittently in conversations not pertinent to the operation of the aircraft for about 15 minutes prior to impact. These conversations covered a number of subjects, from politics to used cars, and both crewmembers expressed strong views and mild aggravation concerning the subjects discussed. The Safety Board believes that these conversations were distractive and reflected a casual mood and lax cockpit atmosphere which continued throughout the remainder of the approach and which contributed to the accident. The overall lack of cockpit discipline was manifested in a number of respects, the Board said, where the flightcrew failed to adhere to recommended or required procedures.

The Board noted that at 0732:13 the flightcrew commenced a discussion of Carowinds Tower, a lighted structure in an amusement park ahead. This discussion lasted 35 seconds, and during this time a considerable degree of the flightcrew's attention was directed outside the cockpit. This particular distraction assumes significance, the Board said, because it was during this period that the DC–9, while still short of Ross Intersection, descended below the 1800 feet mean sea level altitude, or the 1074 feet above the airport altitude, which should have been maintained until after it crossed Ross Intersection.

The Board also noted that at 0733:24, as the aircraft passed over Ross, the flight data recorder showed it was at 1350 feet mean sea level altitude or 624 feet above the airport—which meant it was 450 feet below the prescribed crossing altitude. The FDR on Flight 212 also revealed that the aircraft crossed Ross Intersection at an airspeed of 168 knots instead of the recommended airspeed of 122 knots for its weight at this point. However, the captain did not make the required callout at Ross which should have included the altitude above the airport and any deviation from the recommended approach airspeed.

The Board said that evidence obtained from the cockpit voice recorder also revealed that at 0732:41, during the latter part of the Carowinds Tower discussion, the terrain warning alert sounded in the cockpit, signifying that the DC–9 was 1000 feet above the ground. This warning should have been particularly significant to the flightcrew since it would have made them aware that the aircraft had prematurely descended through the final approach fix at Ross of 1074 feet altitude above the airport elevation. Obviously, the Board said, the crew was not so alerted, since the descent continued.

Commenting on this situation the Board said that, based on pilot testimony taken at the public hearing at Charlotte, it appears that the crew's disregard of the terrain warning signal in this instance may be indicative of the attitudes of many other pilots who regard the signal as more of a nuisance than a warning. If this is the case, the Board believes that airline pilots should re–examine their attitudes toward the terrain warning alert lest the purpose for which the device was installed be defeated.

The Board added that the captain not only failed to make the required callout on altitude and airspeed over Ross Intersection, but shortly after crossing Ross he failed to make the required callout as the aircraft passed through 500 feet above airport elevation; and again failed to make the required callout when the aircraft descended through an altitude of 100 feet above the minimum descent altitude—which is 394 feet above the airport elevation . . . .

On October 8, 1974, the Board issued two safety recommendations to the FAA (A–74–85 and A–74–86) to initiate ways and means to improve professional standards among pilots. These recommendations cited five previous air carrier approach accidents as examples of a casual acceptance of the flight environment, and added that the Charlotte crash reflects once again serious lapses in expected professional conduct. The FAA agreed with both recommendations and is in the process of establishing a working liaison on this subject with both airline management and air carrier pilot organizations.

Airline pilots, as you can imagine, are incensed at the insinuations and accusations contained in this commentary by the NTSB. Charges of complacency and nonprofessionalism are enough to raise anyone's ire to the exploding point, and we're not going to become embroiled in that.

But after reading the above excerpts and boiling over at the Safety Board for making the indictment, each of us should privately ask himself if he has ever been guilty as charged.

We, of course, can't answer for you, but almost every pilot can recall shooting a duck–soup approach during which procedures were abused if not outright ignored. Such lapses in professionalism can be extremely difficult to avoid, and they occur most often when the weather situation is interesting rather than ugly.

Approaches in a broken–cloud condition with good visibilities reported on the surface do most to try a pilot's resolve to fly properly. The ground is in view most of the time, and he expects to break out at 400 to 600 feet with the airport wide open. So he tends to just let the aircraft mosey on down towards the MDA, more or less on the localizer or VOR radial.

If the pilot sees something interesting through a break, the temptation is strong for him to point it out to someone else—the copilot maybe—and discuss it a bit. That's essentially what the crew of the Charlotte DC–9 was doing.

Unfortunately, there are few graphic and convincing examples one can give to convince pilots that that sort of discussion is bad and sometimes deadly. We would go so far as to follow the NTSB's lead and say it is unprofessional. If you want to live long, passage of the initial approach fix must be your signal to stop the small talk and get down to business.

When you stop to think about it, a pilot really earns his pay from the initial inbound, so it's a small thing to be absolutely professional for that short while.

The Non–Thinkers (August 1973)

In studying NTSB statistics year after year, we find that the reason why business and corporate pilots have accidents has not changed appreciably. The percentages caused by poor landing techniques, continued VFR into IFR conditions and maintenance are about the same. The total number of accidents attributed to business and corporate aviation is increasing, but that in itself is not cause for panic, because the number of aircraft being used in business flying is on a sharp increase, so we must expect that the number of accidents attributed to business aviation will trend upward. What is disturbing about the comparison is much more subtle than numbers or percentages.

In a study we once made, there was an accident category called "Doing Something Stupid." This was a list of accident causes ranging from shutting down the engine with the hydraulic pump on it, and so losing power steering and brakes, to forgetting the gear. Those might be termed routinely stupid accidents—Murphy's Law. A year ago they ran just under 10 percent of the total. In a follow-up study, that category was down to 8 percent. But an undercurrent of stupidity that was not present before runs through all of the other categories. This has to be of great concern to us all, because it indicates a growing attitude problem.

Under maintenance, for instance, a pilot at Denver took off in a Cessna 310 and crashed because the aileron cables had been reversed. He was unhurt and probably stormed into the hangar and blamed the mechanic. But we've all been told from our first hour of dual to check both control freedom and the direction of movement. Reversing the cables during maintenance is not uncommon. Cables are often disconnected for something as simple as installing an antenna. In this age of powered controls and auto–trim, we must also remember that it's possible to get the wires or hydraulic lines crossed. After each time a mechanic has been near the airplane, therefore, it's a good idea to run all the controls through full cycle, including the trim tabs, to be certain they follow commands properly. One can't be too thorough in this check. The NTSB reports that another pilot, in a King Air, lost an engine, feathered it, then pulled the firewall shutoff valve and lost the other engine. The valves had been misplacarded.

Double checking the mechanic's work isn't enough by itself. The pilot must also do something about discrepancies, or at least refuse to fly the airplane until it's properly repaired. A corporate pilot, age 47, ATR and 4720 hours, took off in a single–engine aircraft knowing that the fuel selector was not operating correctly. He tried to switch tanks over rough, uneven terrain. The valve hung, and the engine stopped. He and his two passengers walked away from the crash, and we can only hope the boss was screaming, "You're fired!"

In the IFR approach category, a Beech Baron pilot with 1430 total hours tried a nonprecision approach to an airport in fog and missed. Instead of pulling out and going somewhere with an ILS (the ceiling was 300 feet), he tried a VOR approach to a nearby airport that was also reporting below IFR minimums. He busted the MDA and crashed into a river.

Every year, we can depend on this type of accident accounting for about five percent of all of the total business aviation fatalities. There are a dozen reasons why instrument–rated pilots descend below the MDA, push on VFR into IFR conditions, dive or turn sharply for the runway when breaking out too high or off center, and lose control when trying to circle too tightly. The chief reason, however, is a lack of discipline compounded by a lack of preplanning. If more businessmen would admit that a missed approach is not only possible but likely, and make alternate *business* plans, as well as alternate airport plans, the pressure to get down would decrease.

Speaking of pressure, the number of accidents due to the pressures of being a successful businessman as well as a pilot seem to be on the rise. This is an easy trap to fall into. The businessman aviator is often up early and airborne at sunrise to make a 10 A.M. meeting; he then paddles home late at night still thinking about the day's business successes and failures.

101

No one knows how many accidents are caused by this type of fatigue, because they're normally covered up by a secondary cause. In studying the NTSB accident briefs, one finds hints of this. A Texas businessman, for instance, with 8500 total hours flew into the ground in a sand and dust storm—the time was 2045 on an early spring evening. A Georgia businessman with 3400 hours in type totaled an Aztec in a bad landing—time, 0315. A North Carolina businessman with 564 hours in type failed to lower his gear—time 2115 on a winter night.

We can but surmise that fatigue was a contributing cause if not *the* cause in these accidents. In the latest NTSB report, however, there were two accidents to businessmen that were certainly caused by fatigue. An Aztec pilot landed his battered airplane in Kentucky early one morning and admitted that he'd fallen asleep, hit some wires and a tree, woke up, and continued to his destination. Another pilot departed Houston early one morning with a passenger, flew all day, then about 10 at night turned the airplane over to his passenger and went to sleep. The passenger flew into a hilltop.

In total, these stupid-stupidity accidents accounted for 10 percent of those attributed to business and corporate aviation in the NTSB release of briefs. That tempers the overall improvement in the safety record considerably. Evidently, efforts to train pilots better and to give them improved equipment are beginning to pay off. The problem now is how to make pilots think better; how to improve their professional attitude.

ATC   8

Whether the ocean is water or air, millennia
of experience have taught us that the
captain of a vessel is master of his own
fate. When we forget that, safety suffers.

No Help From Below (November 1977)

Two recently released preliminary reports by the NTSB again
prove an old truth: The captain is the captain is the captain.

In today's ATC environment we tend to forget that. Controllers
issue crisp orders with never a "By your leave, Sir" or "If you
concur, Sir" or even a "Please, Sir." Not that there's any time for
such niceties on the frequency, but the tone of ATC's commands
grows more and more authoritarian.

As a result, some pilots have been forgetting that the man on
the ground is a public servant, a mere separator of air traffic. Most
controllers do put more than that into their jobs—we've all been
helped by a controller at one time or another—but a pilot must
never, never get the idea that controllers are omniscient.

If you believe that controllers unfailingly will keep you from
flying into a mountain or will lead you to the nearest airport when
you've got a problem aloft, think again. In 1977, two jet aircraft
crews discovered the realities in the hardest possible way.

The first crew was flying a Learjet out of Palm Springs, California. The accident involved received international notoriety, because one of the passengers was Frank Sinatra's mother.

The NTSB's sketchy preliminary report on this accident leaves the details fuzzy, but this much is certain. The crew departed on Runway 30, hence on a heading of 300 degrees, with a clearance to Las Vegas via the Palm Springs and Twentynine Palms VORTACs. To do that, they should have turned right shortly after takeoff since the Palm Springs VORTAC is abeam and about 4.5 nm northeast of Runway 30.

Since neither the SID nor their departure instructions specified *when* that right turn was to be made (How many times have you been confused by a similar lack of turn instructions on a departure?), and since they were in mountainous terrain, the crew evidently thought that departure control would tell them when it would be safe to make the turn after radar contact was established. So they climbed straight ahead toward their 9000–foot altitude restriction—no doubt feeling uneasy because they'd flown out of Palm Springs before and knew that there are some very high mountains immediately northwest of the airport.

Instructions from the controller added to the confusion. Shortly after liftoff the crew was told to "report crossing 051 radial 10–mile fix."

Note what that could mean to you: You'd be watching for the crossing of the 051 degree radial. But actually what the controller meant was "report established on the 051 degree radial and 10 DME northeast of Palm Springs."

That's quite different, isn't it?

By this time, the crew was obviously quite confused and concerned. Just before leveling at 9000, a crewman asked ATC if they were cleared "via" the 051 degree radial to Twentynine Palms. The controller said yes, but added, "I had a change of route there. Maintain 9000, I'll keep you advised."

In that situation what would you think? You assume you're in a radar environment (In fact, there was no radar at Palm Springs at the time of this accident.), and since no turn instructions have been given, you assume you should continue straight ahead. You're nervous about it, but the controller has told you (as you understood it, at least) to report "crossing" the radial you should intercept; then he's said, "I had a change of route there."

Confusion upon confusion. You try once more to get some help from him. Level at 9000, this Learjet crew told the controller they were heading "three one zero" and asked, "What's our clearance from here?"

The controller missed the significance of that, and the aircraft impacted in the high mountains that lie just 20 miles straight out from Runway 30.

No one can *blame* the controller for this accident. Certainly we do not. The point is, however, that ATC grabs us by the nose and jerks us this way and that so often we tend to forget who is really in charge.

It's quite evident that this crew realized they were flying into trouble, but they *thought* ATC was in command of the situation, so the captain never picked up his mike and said to the controller —as he most certainly should have—"Charlie, I don't know what you have in mind, but there's a mountain up here, so I'm turning northeast and climbing like hell while you figure it out."

A second crew that didn't get any help from below in 1977 when their lives depended on it was flying a Southern DC–9 that crashed in Georgia following a double flameout.

The transcripts of the ATC and cockpit voice recorder tapes on this accident are beyond belief. Even after the crew announced that they'd lost both engines and had a cracked windshield, ATC continued to work other traffic on the frequency. Finally, four minutes and 14 seconds after first telling the controller that they had a major problem, the exasperated first officer came up on the frequency and said, "All right, listen, we've lost both engines, and, uh, I can't, uh, tell you the implications of this, uh, we uh, only got two engines . . . "

The crew was trying to get ATC to vector them to the nearest airport. The controller's solution was to point them at Dobbins Air Force Base, 20 nm to the east of their position. Even in optimum conditions, 20 nm is a long way for a DC–9 at 14,000 feet to glide with both engines out. The conditions, however, were hardly optimum. The airliner was in a thunderstorm at the time. The windshield was cracked and ATC was giving the crew a change in frequency as well as giving other aircraft vectors, altimeter settings, frequency changes, and even ILS frequencies—all on the same frequency.

The DC–9 didn't make it. Again, the controllers should not be blamed. Remember, the captain is the captain is the captain. Of course, almost no one nowadays thinks about losing all the power in a twin jet, but obviously it does happen. In fact several years ago, a captain lost all *four* engines in an air carrier jet. (He was lucky and got them going again.) One must also consider that in any airplane any number of things *can* happen that will force you to land on the nearest airport.

Fire is one. A number of years ago, an airline captain landed a DC–6 at Bryce Canyon, Utah with four engines running but the belly dripping flames. One night a few years later, a captain put a Convair into the unlighted Cushing, Oklahoma airport with a disintegrating engine. More recently, a 707 captain landed his aircraft at an Air Force base with an engine and an entire outer wing panel missing.

Those accidents and ATC's handling of the Southern DC–9 make for a very clear message: The captain had better be prepared to find his own airport should the necessity ever arise. (Ironically, the Southern DC–9 was right over an airport with an IFR approach when the problem developed.)

In fact, whatever your problem may be—a mountain up ahead,

a total power failure, a fire, or just general uneasiness—remember what the rule is: The captain is the captain is the captain. And don't count on any help from below.

Say Again, Clearance Delivery (February 1978)

Most ATC controllers are very sharp, and rarely have we met one who wasn't a professional in the truest sense. But we've got to make the point once again. If a pilot puts all his trust in the ATC system and its personnel, he's going to end up in big trouble.

One aircraft accident report from the NTSB makes the point even more strongly than the incidents just cited. Briefly, the facts are as follows:

In January 1977, the pilot of a Cessna 421 was preparing to depart Nogales, Arizona for Fresno, California. He had flown out of Nogales several times before and was apparently familiar with the IFR departure procedure and should have been familiar with the surrounding high terrain.

He contacted the Tucson FSS by radio from the ground at Nogales and filed direct to the Flats Intersection to intercept Victor 66, as specified in the departure procedure for Nogales. But the FSS specialist said he couldn't find Flats on his map, and so he added, "I don't know if we can get this Flats into the computer or not."

The specialist then told the pilot, "We'd have to put Nogales direct Tucson . . . however the controller would . . . cut you across the corner and take you on V–66 after you contact him. . . . "

The pilot said fine and the clearance came back "cleared as filed to maintain 10,000." After takeoff, he flew directly toward Tucson —as he had filed at the "suggestion" of the FSS specialist and as he was cleared.

After contacting the Tucson departure controller, he was told to maintain VFR and climb to 11,000. He told the controller he couldn't do both, so he was recleared to 10,500 to maintain VFR.

A minute later the pilot told the controller that he couldn't maintain VFR at 10,000. The controller—who still didn't have him radar contact—said that he couldn't approve IFR at that low altitude. The pilot responded that he would have to descend to maintain VFR.

All this time the controller thought the pilot was flying the specified departure procedure from Nogales toward the north- west—toward Flats Intersection—rather than direct Tucson, as he had been cleared. Why the controller thought that, and why he didn't confirm it sooner is unclear. When he finally got the 421 in radar contact, the aircraft was on a heading of 360 degrees— toward a mountain peak just five miles distant.

The controller told the pilot, "Turn left immediately, heading 180 degrees, maintain VFR."

What happened after that can only be conjectured. Evidently, in trying to turn immediately, and stay VFR as well, the pilot lost control of the aircraft. He and his one passenger were killed in the crash.

In summing up, the NTSB wrote, "The National Transportation Safety Board determines that the probable cause of the accident was the controller's issuance of an improper departure clearance, climb restriction and altitude clearance. The controller's lack of knowledge and noncompliance with standard ATC procedures placed the aircraft in proximity to high terrain and the pilot lost control of the aircraft for unknown reasons while executing an emergency controller–directed turn.

"Contributing to the accident were (1) the inadequacy of official guidelines concerning the use of published IFR departure proce- dures, (2) the failure of the departure controller to provide appro- priate services, (3) the inability of the flight service specialist to insert the pilot's requested departure route into the ATC flight data computer, and (4) *the failure of the pilot to check the new*

108

departure clearance and route for proper terrain clearance altitudes." (Italics ours.)

No one can blame the controllers totally for this one. The pilot erred seriously. He trusted the ATC system and the people in it too far. ATC controllers will no doubt become incensed by that statement, saying we are breeding a mistrust that will destroy the very foundations of the ATC system.

We don't think so. The mistrust we advocate is a healthy one —especially for pilots and their passengers. We're not suggesting there should be an adversary relationship between pilots and controllers—that most certainly would destroy the ATC system. But a pilot can take what a controller tells him with a grain of salt without exchanging blows, or even getting into an argument.

It's not a question of argument anyway. It's a matter of flying the airplane safely, and *telling* the controller what you're doing. It's then up to him to persuade you to conduct the flight in a manner that you're not *certain* is safe based on the information you have.

The accident described above illustrates the point well. First, the pilot knew there was a departure procedure for Nogales and he should have followed it unless ATC gave him a very good reason for doing something different.

The inability of the FSS specialist to get Flats Intersection into the computer was the specialist's problem, not the pilot's. If the FSS specialist insisted that the paperwork had to go Nogales direct Tucson, okay, file it that way. But the pilot should have flown the published departure and *told* the controller that he was doing so, the flight plan direct Tucson notwithstanding.

In fact, the controller's own handbook says that's what the pilot should have done. It states, "If a published IFR departure procedure is not included in an ATC clearance, compliance with such a procedure is the pilot's prerogative and responsibility."

Second, the pilot was issued an IFR clearance, so when the

controller told him to maintain VFR, he should have replied that he wasn't going to do that. Both the controller's handbook and AIM are clear on this point—a controller may not tell a pilot on an IFR clearance to remain VFR. A pilot can *ask* to remain VFR, but a controller cannot command it.

Had this pilot *told* the controller he was climbing to 11,000 feet in IMC, as cleared IFR, he would still be alive. The mountain he hit tops out at 9453 feet.

System Errors (July 1973)

In April of 1973, a NASA Convair 990 and a Navy P-3C Orion collided on short approach to Runway 32 Right at Moffett Field, California. Sixteen men died and NASA lost a valuable research airplane.

The NTSB labeled the cause as ATC error: "At initial contact with the control tower (operated by Navy personnel), the 990 was cleared to continue for Runway 32 Right. At seven miles, the Convair 990 was again cleared to continue approach for the right runway. About three miles out, the control tower operator cleared the Convair to land on Runway 32 *Left*. The Convair pilot acknowledged the new runway assignment. The control tower operator also cleared the P-3C to continue his approach to Runway 32 Left. It was the tower operator's intention to land the Convair 990 on Runway 32 Right, but he mistakenly called the wrong runway."

The collision was one of the rare ones at a controlled airport, but the potential for similar accidents is becoming quite common. I was once told to continue straight in for 17 Left at Memphis International when I heard the tower clear an American Airlines flight to land on 35 Right. Before I could get on the horn, the AA captain protested and got it sorted out.

The controller had meant to give him *35 Left*.

110

A few days later we departed Teterboro, actual IFR, behind a Cherokee and got vectors to Solberg VOR identical to those given to the Cherokee pilot. He was cleared to 9000 and we to 10,000. Approaching Solberg, it became apparent that the controller was having a problem. He asked us each for repeated idents and altitude checks. When the Cherokee finally reported Solberg climbing through 7000 feet, we were 3.5 DME *beyond* Solberg going through 8000. Somewhere back there we had crossed both paths and altitudes.

The next day, again in actual IFR, we were working departure at 5000 feet, heading 240, with a faster aircraft coming up on our right also at 5000, when the controller asked us to turn *right* to 200. In a terminal area it's not unusual to be asked to turn the long way around, but fortunately we had been paying attention and we questioned the controller. He corrected himself and asked us to turn *left* to 200 degrees *for spacing.*

We shouldn't berate the ATC profession for these incidents. Controllers are invariably professionals, but they are also human and often overloaded—particularly in high–density areas—and frequently they must work with imperfect equipment.

We pilots sometimes add to their problems. Crossing Little Rock, Arkansas one day, we heard ATC tell a departing DC–9 below us to turn left to 190, then watched him turn right. When the controller asked where he was going, a crewman replied, "Oops, I painted the wrong thumb red this morning."

The point of all this, of course, is that the IFR pilot in today's IFR environment must be more thoroughly aware and more unquestionably professional than ever before. Once upon a time we could listen for our own call sign and tune everything else out. Nowadays it's necessary to hear everything and to visualize what everyone else on the frequency is doing in relation to us.

This is awareness. What one *does* with awareness is the measure of professionalism. We have heard some pilots short circuit

ATC and begin talking directly with other aircraft on the frequency after a mistake has been discovered. That can only lead to chaos. Other pilots begin to second guess the controller, which may lead to anarchy.

Normally it is enough to be aware and to exercise the appropriate caution. When that is not enough, then all we can do in a radar–based system is to call the problem to the controller's attention and help him work it out.

MAINTENANCE 9

In the pursuit of excellence in aviation
safety we must occasionally pause to recall
that the burden lies not on pilots and ATC
controllers alone. The mechanic too has a
crucial responsibility.

Poor Maintenance as the Cause (January 1978)

Poor maintenance has long been too often a cause of accidents,
and now it seems to be more prevalent. Most mechanics are
skilled, dedicated, conscientious individuals, and the man with an
A&P certificate in his hip pocket can be proud of it. But there are
the less dedicated kind out there as well.

We have examined a release of NTSB accident briefs for 1976
and have broken out all the accidents in which a mechanical or
inspection failure was a cause or contributing factor. We are
shocked at the numbers. Of 898 accidents, 206, or 22 percent, can
be classed as "mechanicals" of one sort or another. This is from
just one summary of NTSB briefs. For the full year, there must
be about 1000 mechanical accidents.

Not all of those can be charged to a mechanic. Among the 206
accidents from this particular summary are 38 engine failures for
reasons undetermined. Some of those are no doubt carburetor
icing incidents. Others are *probably* (the briefs don't give enough

detail to say for certain) pilot–induced failures for reasons ranging from allowing engines to load up in glides to forgetting to
push mixtures in during descents.

Another 23 of the 206 mechanical accidents must definitely be
charged to the pilot. Several, for example, were no more serious
than an inoperative starter—until the pilot hand cranked the airplane, and it taxied away without him.

In several other instances, pilots noted a maintenance discrep-
ancy and attempted flight without even talking to a mechanic.
Let's look at some examples:

• Pilot noted right brake weak before takeoff. Right brake
failed on landing. Master cylinder leaking internally.

• Gear collapsed on landing. Shock struts were bottomed out
during preflight.

• Right flap inoperative. Time of failure unknown. Pilot reported no flight control problems.

• Pilot–in–command attempted operation with known deficiencies in equipment. Pilot stated that an old kink in the carburetor
heat cable probably separated.

Obviously, the best A&P ever certificated can't do anything to
prevent those kinds of accidents. But another group of 33 mishaps
turned up in our study that fall into a gray area. These were
accidents resulting from material failures, most of them in an
engine or vital engine accessory.

Whether or not a good mechanic could have prevented these
incidents and accidents is questionable. In some cases it appears
that a mechanic didn't get a chance simply because the aircraft
owner didn't take his airplane to a shop for proper inspections. In
other cases it appears that the owner might have been getting by
with the cheapest maintenance possible. When you seek out the
lowest priced shop, you're actually seeking trouble.

In still other cases among these 33 accidents we suspect that a little extra effort on the part of some mechanic might have prevented a lot of grief:

• Ball–joint fitting on throttle separated causing a partial loss of power. The aircraft hit a greenhouse and the pilot and two of his three passengers were seriously injured. This was a relatively new aircraft—a Piper Arrow in the N–number suffix T series—so it was probably getting maintenance attention more or less regularly. Did a mechanic fail to inspect that ball–joint properly? Every time the cowling is off for an oil change, things like that can and should be looked over.

• Following the crash of a Beech Baron, investigators discovered that "numbers two, four and six cylinders on the right engine were full of oil and the plugs were oil fouled." It's possible that the owner grossly overheated this engine, causing the piston rings to lose their temper. But it's also possible that a mechanic wasn't as careful as he should have been when performing the last compression check.

• Fatigue fracture, throttle power lever assemblies, attempted go–around, lost manifold pressure, started to turn back to runway and crashed in fuel dump. Two of four people onboard were seriously injured. This too was a relatively new aircraft, a Rockwell 112A. Did a mechanic overlook a misaligned throttle linkage that was certain to fatigue?

• Number six cylinder failed at the base flange on the Continental O–300 in a 1966 Cessna Skyhawk. A base flange failure is often the result of either loose hold–down nuts or uneven tightening during a reinstallation. It's a fatigue situation, so a mechanic who discovers two or more loose nuts on one side of a cylinder base should be very suspicious. He should, in fact, demand that the cylinder come off for a thorough inspection or replacement.

• Number two cylinder rocker shaft bosses failed and the student pilot on a solo flight undershot the forced landing. That type

115

of failure is often the result of using the wrong method for driving the rocker shaft out during an overhaul or dropping the cylinder during replacement.

The part the mechanic played in all of the above accidents is uncertain, but that's not always so. From the 206 accidents in this study, we have broken out 84—9.4 percent of the total 898 accidents that occurred in this period—which must be charged off to outright poor and shoddy maintenance.

We've broken these 84 accidents into two groups: those resulting from inadequate inspection practices and techniques and those resulting from downright inept performance on the part of a mechanic. Let's look at some examples in that first group:

• MU–2B being operated in corporate/executive service—After touchdown, the gear retracted for no apparent reason. There were no injuries. Investigation disclosed that a wire from the gear selector switch had been chafing. Eventually the insulation wore through, and arcing occurred four inches from the switch causing the gear to retract. It's not easy to lie on your back with an inspection mirror and look at everything behind the panel, but in this instance, it would have prevented substantial damage to an expensive airplane.

• Bell 47J–2A used in commercial service—On a sightseeing flight with four passengers onboard, the tail rotor pinion gear failed due to lack of lubrication. Two fatalities and three serious injuries were the result. The NTSB cited the ground crew as having improperly serviced the aircraft. The pilot, of course, should have caught the low oil level during his preflight, but pilots make mistakes too.

• Piper Cherokee operated for personal transportation by a private owner—The oil line to the oil cooler deteriorated to the point of rupture, and the aircraft was substantially damaged in a forced landing. The NTSB lists the probable cause as inadequate maintenance and inspection. It seems unreasonable to us that an oil line would deteriorate to the point of failure between one annual inspection and the next. Someone just didn't inspect carefully enough.

• Cessna 210 being used for dual instruction—Hydraulic downline for main gear worn through by chafing. The NTSB blamed inadequate maintenance and inspection.

• Erco 415–C being flown by an 18–year–old pleasure pilot—The NTSB found that the "left aileron control cable failed at the control quadrant; 43 hours since the last inspection."

We could go on and on for 43 accidents—about one in 21 of all general aviation accidents—in which poor inspection was a cause. But far more important than any of the above were 41 other accidents in which the mechanic was directly at fault. Remember, these are from a group of 898 accidents that appear in just one of five summaries the NTSB released in one year.

Before looking at the myriad ways in which mechanics have erred, we must mention some interesting generalizations. First, when a mechanic goofs, people seldom get seriously hurt. In these 41 accidents, only six people were killed and another eight seriously injured. In fact, only eight of the 41 aircraft were destroyed. The other 33 were substantially damaged. But that has to be small consolation to the mechanics involved, because they really did a bunch of dumb things:

• Piper Arrow being flown by a private pilot—"Mechanics failed to properly install a magneto and left a nut loose on the number three connecting rod during overhaul." Not much can be added to that excerpt from NTSB records.

• Boelkow BO–105 helicopter used in commercial air taxi service—"Cotter pin securing nut on lower tail rotor bell–crank bolt not installed after reassembly." Again, what else can be said?

• Cessna 188 being used to spray chemicals—"Failure of propeller hub assembly . . . . Noncompliance with McCauley service bulletin 110."

117

• Piper Comanche on a post maintenance flight test—The engine failed when the gear was extended because, "when lowering the gear the nose gear door right center hinge bolt hung up on throttle cable. Wrong bolt, inadequate clearance."

• Cessna 206 being flown by a businessman pilot—"Seats improperly secured; seat slid rearward on takeoff because the safety stop was missing." In this instance the pilot was at fault because he should have ensured that the seat was locked. But, as mentioned earlier, pilots also err. There are 10 or 12 accidents each year resulting from safety stops not being replaced after the mechanic has had a seat out for some reason. In another of these accidents, the seat slid forward enough for the front runners to leave the tracks. Then, during the landing, the seat tipped rearward causing the pilot to lose control in the rollout. He was seriously injured, and the aircraft was destroyed.

• Piper Arrow being flown for personal transportation——"Oil exhaustion as a result of improper engine oil quick drain valve installation." Two people were seriously injured as a result of this too–prevalent goof. It's very well known that the nose gear on a number of single–engine retractables will open the oil quick drain unless it's positioned just right. The potential for that should be checked every time the cowling is off and certainly every time any maintenance is performed that might change the position of the valve or of the retracted nose gear.

• Bell 47D–1 on a test flight following maintenance——"Tail rotor rigged in reverse." That's another common cause of accidents. Normally it's the aileron cables that are reversed, but we once witnessed a mechanic and a pilot in a heated argument over which way an elevator trim tab should go when the trim wheel is rolled back. The pilot was right and knew he was right because he'd just landed from a very interesting flight of the aircraft—which was a DC–6. In this group of 41 accidents that directly resulted from improper maintenance, we didn't find an incident

118

quite like that. But one mechanic did fail to reconnect a trim tab rod after tab maintenance on a Cessna 421. The corporate/executive pilot walked away from the accident, but the airplane was substantially damaged.

• Cessna T210G on a flight for personnel transportation with three onboard—"Vacuum lines to instruments found one–half to one and one–half turns loose from finger tight." The pilot was evidently a couple of hours into the flight when he lost the attitude instruments, became spatially disoriented, and pulled the airplane apart while recovering from an unusual attitude.

On the basis of this one study, it's difficult to say positively that maintenance incidents are on the increase, but there are indications to that effect. And small wonder. Aircraft become more sophisticated each year, but both mechanics' salaries and the pool of highly skilled people who were trained for the Big War of 1941-1945 are decreasing.

To correct this problem, mechanics must be trained better in the beginning, with emphasis on inspection techniques and follow–up inspections. Then the better ones must be paid more to keep them from leaving airports for jobs in local auto shops.

By the way, to prove that we're sincere when we say the mechanic shouldn't be blamed for *everything*, we'll end with this one:

Following an accident due to an engine failure in a Cessna 172, investigators tore the carburetor down. The result was this terse remark by the NTSB: "Two dead mice found lodged in the carburetor venturi."

SELECTIONS   10

Each year the National Transportation
Safety Board releases its probable cause
for each of more than 4000 aviation
accidents. We can learn much by breaking
them into select groups for comparative
study.

Selected Accidents: Summer and Fall 1976 (September 1977)

Every now and again, it's educational to browse through the
NTSB's lists of recent accidents to see how we're doing and, more
important, *what* we're doing.

Last year the record for business and corporate/executive operators was still holding up quite well. Exposure figures aren't
available, except by wild guess, nor are the totals in, so rates
cannot be given yet. But comparisons with other segments of
general aviation can be made.

Based on about 1000 accidents in the period for which a cause
has been determined, business operators, (including the cor-
porate/executive segment), are experiencing 7.3 percent of the
total accidents. That compares to 50.9 percent for pleasure fliers,
and 11.7 in training operations. Air taxi operations account for
about 4.2 percent of the total.

When fatal accidents are compared, the business sector is involved in only five percent of the total, compared to 66.9 for the private sector, 11.5 for training, and 8.8 in air taxi operations.

One can never be proud of an accident record unless it is zero, but business aviation can be less ashamed of the record than any other major sector in general aviation. We must hang our heads over some of the individual accidents, however.

• Ever since airplanes have had two engines and feathering props, stories about pilots feathering the wrong one have been rife in aviation, and it's still happening. Last year the guilty party was a young man with 2600 total hours. He was on a business trip in a Cessna 310 with two passengers. The left engine lost a lot of oil and began to run rough. The airplane was in cruise, so there was no hurry, but the pilot feathered the *right* prop, whereupon the left engine quit entirely. The pilot tried for an airport, put the gear out too soon, saw he wasn't going to make the runway, brought the gear up again, and still touched down short. Everyone fortunately walked away.

• This example can be taken with a grain of salt. Out in West Texas, this businessman pilot did something to make a competitor very, very angry. He was flying along in his Cessna 310 one day when suddenly both engines failed. He landed off airport, gear up, and walked away. An inspection disclosed that someone had poured table salt into his fuel tanks.

• The most bizarre accident of the period has been well publicized. A G–II was taxiing to a parking area, and the tail contacted a 7200–volt powerline. The voltage, seeking a ground through the airframe, caused a fire in a wheel assembly. In the ensuing confusion a lineman and one crewman were electrocuted.

Those three were the unusual accidents on the record. They were so unusual, they teach us little. Education comes from a study of routine accidents, and what is more routine, or commonplace than busting a landing? In the summer and fall of 1976,

121

there was a long string of those. Here are some of the more interesting ones:

• The pilot of a pressurized Beech Baron arrived in rain over the destination airport, a 2500–foot grass strip. According to the flight manual landing chart (Beech does give one for a grass runway), he needed a minimum of 2300 feet to land the 58P on *dry* grass. The chart doesn't give a correction factor for wet grass, but if 2300 feet are needed on dry grass, you don't have to be Smiling Jack to guess that an extra 200 feet isn't enough of a margin on a wet surface.

Our hero didn't think about any of this. He and his passengers walked away, but the new Baron was substantially damaged in the ditches beyond the far end of the runway.

The lesson is very clear. The flight manual should always be consulted before landing on a short runway. If the runway is short, grass, *and wet,* the flight manual should not just be consulted but studied at great length. Flight manuals almost never give a correction factor for wet versus dry grass, because there are too many variables. But our rule is at least 50 percent additional length for the ground roll portion on a grassy runway. In the case of the 58P, that would dictate a *wet* grass runway of at least 3100 feet in length.

• Here's another one. This grass runway was also wet and at an elevation of 2500 feet. It was a warm day as well, so the density altitude was close to 4000 feet. If the pilot of the 310 had studied his flight manual and added our fudge factor, he would have discovered that he needed a minimum of 2100 feet to get stopped. That was okay, because he had 3125 feet of runway.

But the 2100 feet in the 310 charts assumes a well–executed approach and touchdown. This 1000–hour pilot—320 in type—approached high and hot and wouldn't go around. No one was injured, but the 310 became a mess.

Again, the lesson is clear and almost too fundamental to stress.

It's not enough *just to consult* the landing charts; you must also execute.

• Landing long on short runways doesn't make up the full extent of the errors in landing judgment. Last summer a young businessman pilot with 400 hours attempted a night landing on a lighted gravel runway in Washington state. He did a fair job, but he let the aircraft drift left a bit and it fell into a ditch. As it turned out, the ditch was *inside* the runway boundary lights.

This just goes to show that night landings should be made at strange airports with great caution. We learned that one night on a steep approach to an unfamiliar runway when trees showed up in the landing lights. Next morning we discovered that our approach had been just steep enough to clear a high, wooded hill in the approach path.

• General aviation continues to be saddled with accidents that are just plain ridiculous. Some folks out West were looking up at the clouds one day and observed a pressurized Aero Commander come spinning out of the overcast with one engine feathered. Investigation disclosed that the businessman pilot did not have an instrument ticket. How much twin time he had could not be determined.

There's something upsetting about a man who hasn't even got an instrument ticket flying around in a pressurized airplane.

• Speaking of not being qualified, a 58–year-old man with almost 10,000 total hours and 1500 hours in type was twiddling along in a Twin Bonanza. A man that age with all those hours should have been able to handle almost anything. But when an engine stopped, he failed to (1) feather it and (2) put the gear down before touchdown on an airport.

• We should end this with the saga of aviation's luckiest man of 1976. He was a 230–hour pilot and did not have an instrument rating. But that did not deter him from flying his Bonanza into a thunderstorm over the mountains of Nevada. When the storm spit him out, both wings and both ruddervators were bent and twisted beyond repair. He landed on an airport successfully and, we hope, vowed to never do *that* again.

Ninety–Seven Too Many (July 1972)

Five times each year the National Transportation Safety Board issues a compilation of aircraft accident reports that describe the cause and circumstance of from 800 to 1000 mishaps. It's called *Aircraft Accident Reports, Brief Format.* Regrettably, it's *not* brief. Each issue fills nearly 900 pages, and days are required to study and digest it. But time and difficulty notwithstanding, the report is rich in vital information, and we can all profit from a careful analysis of it.

The NTSB's categorization of accidents into various classes of operation makes extracting the useful bits of information somewhat easier. In the edition used for this study, the NTSB has assigned 97 accidents out of a total of 896 to business and executive flying. Corporate pilots were charged with only 22 accidents, which is indeed a good record, but businessmen pilots accounted for 75, and that's not so good.

The NTSB cites pilot error and poor judgment as the greatest single cause of accidents, but to say the pilot erred is of absolutely no use to us. It's like saying the pilot crashed because he had only two arms. The fact is that airplanes crash because pilots fly them into situations calling for more ability than they possess. To prevent repetition of a particular accident, we need a probable cause that tells us which skill was found wanting in a given situation. Only then can we emphasize the correct accident–prevention knowledge and skills in training, refresher courses, and safety literature. We therefore took the accidents in this study and broke them down into 10 types, according to the skill that was tested and proved deficient.

SELECTIONS

• *Landings (20 accidents)*

——Landing continues to be the general aviation pilot's greatest weakness. The 20 accidents of this type resulted from a variety of causes—from improper recovery after a bounced touchdown to landing a turbojet downwind on a short, wet runway. The preponderance of landing accidents were overshoots and ground-loops as a result of wheelbarrowing. This indicates a tendency to be too proud to go around, or perhaps to feel we haven't the time. In either event—to save embarrassment or time—we drive it onto the runway and stand on the brakes. Or, worse still, we wait until it's much too late and then begin a go–around. Since the average time–in–type for landing accidents charged to business flying is 805 hours, one is reluctant to suggest that inadequate initial training is a factor. High time–in–type itself may actually be the problem. It breeds complacency and develops unsafe operating practices.

• *Handling Weather (13 accidents)*

——This one is the killer. One–third of all fatal accidents occur to pilots trying to go VFR in IFR weather. Continued VFR is so deadly that only two pilots in the 13 accidents covered by the study survived. Why do pilots continue to gamble against those odds?

It's customary to write off these weather accidents as classic instances of inexperience or poor judgment, but the average total time of the pilots involved (1215 hours) belies that, and so does the fact that thousands of other pilots who have pushed a lot of weather in uncounted hours of cross–country flying have gotten away with it.

The chief problem is that we are conditioned to be optimistic about weather. The forecast is often bad, but 99 times out of 100,

125

when you go take a look, it's not so bad after all. So you push on, thinking it'll certainly improve in another mile or so. That also explains why two of the 13 pilots involved in this type of accident were instrument rated. Their experience probably told them it would get better, so why bother getting a clearance.

If forecasts of bad weather were more often right than wrong, the incidence of continued–VFR accidents would drop dramatically. But until that happens, we must urge all business pilots to get an instrument rating and use it. It will increase the utility of the airplane by 50 percent and the chances of staying alive manyfold.

• *Takeoffs (11 accidents)*

——Pilot businessmen also display much misplaced optimism about their ability to get out of small airports. Of the 11 takeoff accidents, three occurred in summer months and were due to high density altitudes, one happened during spring as a result of heavy mud, three took place in the winter in heavy snow, two of these planes were on floats, one was a STOL airplane, and one was a helicopter unsuccessfully trying to lift itself out of deep mud.

Obviously, recurrent training is desperately needed. The average time–in–type for the pilots was 360 hours, and if they hadn't learned how much runway an airplane needs after 360 hours of flying it, they probably never would without outside help.

• *Forced Landings (11 accidents)*

——For those who fly in dread of engine failure, it's comforting to discover that nine out of 11 business pilots involved in power–stoppage accidents proved skillful enough to get down in relatively good shape; seven of the 11 walked away with only minor injuries. (Untold numbers, we should add, got down without even

126

bending the aircraft, and so are not mentioned in this study.)

The startling fact is that two–thirds of the engine–out accidents were in twins. Moreover, *all the fatal* engine–out accidents were in twins. Add to that the discovery that four of the seven twin pilots involved in engine–out accidents lost the engine in cruise (the other three lost *both* engines), and one cannot deny that engine–out proficiency is sadly lacking. And this is not confined to low–time twin owners. Those involved had a low of 1700 hours and a high of 11,000. The message is clear: If you fly a twin, frequent practice of engine–out procedures under the guidance of a capable instructor is a must.

• *Maintenance (11 accidents)*

——Most, if not all, of the power–failure accidents discussed above were, in the final analysis, due to improper maintenance. (Fuel exhaustion and misuse of engine controls are covered in other accident categories.) But in addition to those, there were 10 gear–up accidents, wholly or partially due to faulty maintenance, and one case of an elevator turnbuckle being improperly safetied. The 10 gear–up incidents included rusty slide tubes, erratic operation of motors, and histories of a variety of gear problems that had been previously noted but left uncorrected.

It would seem logical to blame mechanics for these accidents, but the fact is that corporate aircraft, which receive regular, systemized maintenance, are rarely involved in accidents caused by mechanical failures. Too many individual owners try to skimp. The FARs require only one annual inspection, and many owners try to get by with that. It just isn't enough. The record shows that if you can't afford to maintain a plane, you can't afford to fly it. Rather than make do with a poorly maintained twin, fly a well–maintained single; it's safer.

CAUSE AND CIRCUMSTANCE

• *Avoiding Doing Something Dumb (10 accidents)*

——This is the group which proves that to err is human. These are the unthinking, ridiculous, stupid accidents that could happen to any of us at any time, no matter how experienced and well trained we may be (as indicated by the number of these accidents that happened to corporate crews with an average total time of 7345 hours). The best that can be done to help prevent recurrences is to list them, in the hope that we will recall someone else's mistake when next we reach for the wrong switch.

The most costly accident in the group occurred when a taxiing JetStar crew shut down number–two and –three engines, forgetting that they were set up for the number–two–engine hydraulic system. With no hydraulics, they had no steering or brakes and hit a parked aircraft. Another crew turned on the cabin heater in a King Air with the blower circuit breaker pulled and melted a mess of ducts.

A 700–hour, single–engine pilot came down from altitude, failed to advance the mixture control, and then stacked it trying to get into a short field with partial power. Another single–engine pilot, this one with 8000 hours, tried to take off in a Cessna 210 with a bolt through the hole drilled in the control wheel shaft and control lock collar. It had been placed there after the standard flagged pin control lock was lost.

The pilot of a twin engaged the autopilot immediately after liftoff and looked away from his instruments. The airplane flew back into the ground. The pilot of another twin experienced a loss of power on the right side during his takeoff run. He retarded the left throttle to abort. Just then the right engine came back to life with a roaring surge, and he groundlooped—with rather expensive results.

And finally, those inevitable gear–up incidents. One pilot simply forgot. Another began his takeoff run with the selector in the up position. A third put the selector up while going through his pre–takeoff checklist.

• *The IFR Approach (four accidents)*

——These four accidents all involved descents below MDA. Only one of them was of the familiar old get–down–no–matter–the–odds variety. Three of the four occurred during nonprecision approaches, two of them at night. A factor in one was a malfunctioning altimeter on the pilot's side. The NTSB does not say if there was a copilot's altimeter installed, but the aircraft was a Queen Air A80, and there probably was. A copilot was aboard and should have been backing up his captain. Another twin pilot, flying solo, acknowledged the local barometric setting, then flew into the trees with his altimeter set 0.24 inches high. The crew of a turboprop descended into trees at night in sleet, freezing rain, and heavy snow. The tower saw the aircraft approaching in level flight with the landing lights on before it settled into the trees. The NTSB says the cause was improper IFR operation, but it's just possible that the crew was unable to maintain MDA due to airframe ice.

The fourth accident occurred when the pilot of a light twin tried to make a steep turn toward the runway rather than execute a missed approach after breaking out under a 500–foot ceiling too far off centerline.

• *Proper Loading (three accidents)*

——Let's face it, just about every pilot with 500 hours or more in his log book has, at one time or another, flown an aircraft loaded over gross. It's neither legal nor smart, but when done with discretion, the risk is minimal. Done indiscriminately, it can lead to unhappy consequences. The most important rule is never to load the aircraft in a manner exceeding the approved CG range. One pilot of a light twin evidently breached that rule. He had a very short trip. The twin lifted off, tried to climb straight up, and stalled.

If you have no option but to overload the aircraft, restrict the load to a modest four or five percent. The pilot of a Cessna Cardinal was a whopping 17 percent over gross when he made a very short trip. Unable to climb over the wires surrounding Toledo's big airport, he tried to abort and came smack up against a telephone pole.

A third rule is, when overloaded, fly with care. The pilot of a medium twin flew 1000 miles overloaded, then, still over gross, he blew a VFR approach to a large airport and stalled out trying to go around. Average time for the three pilots, who should have known better, was 2367 hours.

• *Seeing and Being Seen (two accidents)*

——Pilots who fly several hundred hours each year probably worry more about collisions than anything else. Evidently, the worry and resulting vigilance are paying off, because business aviation was charged with only two such accidents in this study. In one, a pilot, landing into the sun, hit an aircraft holding for takeoff at the edge of the runway. The other, the only midair collision, was between a low–wing Cessna 310 and a high–wing Tripacer. The 310 landed without further incident; the Tripacer did not. The NTSB faulted each pilot equally.

• *Fuel Awareness (two accidents)*

——Powered aircraft fly very poorly on empty tanks, but pilots keep trying. In this study a helicopter pilot with 320 hours in type tried and failed to stretch his fuel to McCarren Field in Las Vegas.

130

He landed just off the airport with a costly *kerthump*. Another pilot did the same thing in a Cessna 172, crunching to a stop just short of the runway at Bishop, California. The rule is, if you think you can just make it, you probably won't. Stop and refuel.

• *Avoiding the Wake (two accidents)*

——This is another hazard we all worry about, but in this case we evidently don't worry nearly enough. There's absolutely no excuse to get upset by a wake. All we have to do is fly above the path of the wake maker.

• *Miscellaneous (eight accidents)*

——These are the weird ones. Three in this group occurred when pilots simply flew into the ground. Two of them were at night over dark terrain, but the third was in VFR daylight. Another accident happened to a pilot who was operating beyond the limits of his medical certificate. A restriction against night flight notwithstanding, he tried a circling approach in three–quarter–mile visibility at night and flew into trees.

A pilot with monocular vision hit a pole near the end of the runway. A Bonanza pilot tried a slow roll in the rarified air over Aspen, Colorado and discovered he wasn't the hot pilot he thought he was.

The final accident occurred to a 485–hour pilot (270 hours in type) after he discovered on his preflight that the elevator trim tab control was inoperative. He took off anyway and then pitched into the ground. To business flying's credit, only one drunken charge was made against business pilots by the NTSB in this accounting.

The common denominator in these accidents is a skill grown dull. Judging by the average total time of the pilots involved, even the weather accidents must be charged to a dulling of the low-

131

time pilot's ability to recognize his limits. Only the odd accident can be charged off to inability. A few might have been caused by inattention to the job at hand, but paying attention itself is a skill. It can be sharpened by following good operating practices, even when everything is going right, and by following the example of the professionals who fly business planes for the corporations. Not a year goes by in which they don't take several proficiency checks. You may not need them, but it's nice to always be a little sharper than necessary.

The extra skill—the reserve ability that comes from constantly following good operating practices and from periodic checks to correct bad habits—is what gets us out of unforecast trouble.

Rare But Lethal (February 1973)

Because of what they can teach us, freak accidents and those that occur due to rare causes ought to be part of the safety thinking of all business and corporate pilots. Let's investigate three of them.

The first involved an aborted instrument approach. Precisely why the go–around in 500–and–one weather ended in tragedy for the twin jet is not known as of this writing, but it's safe to say that it occurred because the airplane or the crew was not prepared for the approach. The chilling thing is that all of us who make a lot of instrument flights probably come within a heartbeat of having an accident for a similar reason several times each year.

The 500–and–one approach is a piece of cake. In fact, after making enough of them, one doesn't even think of 500 and one as a bona fide IFR approach. It's more like a let down and VFR landing. This complacency leads us into all sorts of corners. Several months ago I was with a pilot who closed his Jepp book and threw it onto the back seat after crossing the outer marker. It never occurred to him that he might have need for the missed

132

approach procedure. Last winter, another pilot, arriving at the outer marker quite high, was so certain of landing out of an 800–and–two approach that he pulled off all the power and pushed the nose down. He broke out short, and the chilled engines would not respond. He landed in a field, 500 feet shy of the runway.

There are reasons beyond number why a landing out of *any* approach may not be in the bag. In the accident cited here, the crew was told—just upon breaking out—to go around because a preceding aircraft had not cleared the runway quickly enough. An accident can close an airport instantly, even when you're on final. There have even been instances of pilots breaking out and finding kids on bicycles on the runway.

The point, obviously, is that although it happens rarely, the preceding airplane does occasionally land gear up, or a car drives onto the runway; so we must never let ourselves become mentally or mechanically committed to land until we have actually touched down with a clear runway ahead.

The cause of the second accident in this group is subject to considerable conjecture. The corporate jet involved was departing in VFR conditions. At 800 feet altitude, it suddenly nosed over, banked left, and flew into a tank farm. The cause could have been runaway trim, or elevator control separation, or it could have been crew incapacitation.

There have been a number of accidents over the years as a result of a crewman slumping over the controls during a takeoff or landing. The FAA records an average of five inflight heart attacks in general aviation a year. There are also cases of air carrier pilot incapacitation. The significant thing is that the average age of the individuals involved is 48, and growing numbers of corporate pilots are pushing their mid–50's.

If the incapacitation occurs at altitude, the consequences are relatively minor—except, of course to the stricken individual. At low altitudes, however, the remaining crewman (if a second pilot is aboard), must be both quick and exceedingly strong to prevent a tragedy. Inflight heart attacks, unfortunately, are most likely to happen at low altitudes. The reason for this is well documented. A recent study by the FAA shows that heartbeat rate increases as much as 16 beats per minute as a pilot flies from the outer to the middle marker. Similar stress has been recorded on departures.

The third accident in this trio could easily set off a storm of controversy and recriminations. We're not about to assign a cause here, but the evidence is that a ground controller expected a crew to do one thing and the crew thought they were expected to do something else. This is a trap we all get suckered into much too often.

In this instance, a plane had landed on Runway 14 and rolled out into a quarter–mile fog. In those conditions, you'd be primarily interested in getting out of the way of other traffic on Runway 14; you wouldn't expect a departure on 27. Result: As the crew was taxiing, their aircraft was struck by a departure while crossing 27.

Controllers often act in mysterious ways, and the pilot who tries to second–guess them may just get burned. How many times have you expected ATC to tell you to do one thing but you were actually told to do something else? If you fly with any frequency, it's happened to you, and there undoubtedly have been instances in which you've been so sure of what you *should* have been told to do that you've failed to catch the switch.

A number of procedures will overcome this problem: Always read back instructions whenever getting them right might be crucial. Tell the copilot to *listen*, not *think*, and to ask ATC for clarification whenever the captain apparently heard wrong. A third procedure for preventing accidents due to misunderstanding —and one that could have prevented the accident in question—is never to cross any runway without double checking for traffic by

134

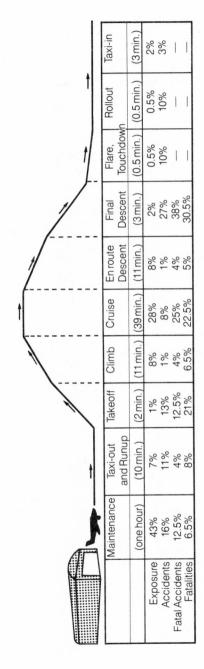

	Maintenance	Taxi-out and Runup	Takeoff	Climb	Cruise	En route Descent	Final Descent	Flare, Touchdown	Rollout	Taxi-in
	(one hour)	(10 min.)	(2 min.)	(11 min.)	(39 min.)	(11 min.)	(3 min.)	(0.5 min.)	(0.5 min.)	(3 min.)
Exposure	43%	7%	1%	8%	28%	8%	2%	0.5%	0.5%	2%
Accidents	16%	11%	13%	1%	8%	1%	27%	10%	10%	3%
Fatal Accidents	12.5%	4%	12.5%	4%	25%	4%	38%	—	—	—
Fatalities	6.5%	8%	21%	6.5%	22.5%	5%	30.5%	—	—	—

(October 1975)

looking or by making a confirming call to the tower.

Honor is never due to a pilot after an accident, but the rarer the cause the more ignominy is attached to it. These three rare ones were easily preventable with advance planning and preparation.

Accidents Versus Phase of Flight (October 1975)

One of the best tools for identifying accident–causing inadequacies is the trip profile. When a random selection of accidents is plotted against this device, the phases of flight that give us the most trouble stand out like a crumpled wing tip.

The one we've developed for corporate/executive operations is illustrated here. It's based on an average trip length of one hour plus 20 minutes, and an average maintenance/service factor of 0.75 manhours per hour of flight. In this instance, we've plotted against the profile all the corporate/executive accidents as compiled by the NTSB for one full year.

The first number shown for each phase of flight is the percentage of total trip time (two hours plus 20 minutes, including the necessary maintenance and service) spent in that phase. The second number is the percentage of total accidents charged to that phase; and, finally, the percentage of deaths charged to each phase.

For the profile to have any meaning, obviously, the accident itself must be charged off against the phase of flight in which it *began*—not the one in which it occurred. For example, a wheels–up landing due to a mechanical failure should be charged to a deficient maintenance skill, although it occurred in the flare and touchdown phase.

Now let's look at each phase individually.

SELECTIONS

• *Maintenance*

——Although only 16 percent of the accidents are charged to maintenance—against 43 percent of the flight actually being spent in the shop—the rate is far too high. Granted, some of these incidents were ultimately the result of the owner or pilot's failure to submit the aircraft for maintenance, and others resulted from undetectable material failures, but the NTSB reports leave no doubt that eight of the 15 incidents in the group would have been prevented had some mechanic or serviceman been as skillful and knowledgeable as he should have been.

• *Taxi–out and Run–up*

——It's difficult to believe that so many accidents happen before the aircraft taxies into takeoff position. Of the 10 accidents charged to this phase, three resulted from the pilot or crew's beginning takeoff with known damage or deficiencies. Two pilots struck objects or chuck holes while taxiing out; the third took off with a dead battery in an airplane with electric gear and flap actuators.

Two other incidents (both in pressurized cabin twins) resulted from allowing passengers to close the rear door—improperly, as it happened. Two more resulted from nonuse of the checklist: One pilot departed with the alternator switches off, and the other failed to turn on the igniters for his turbine engines before departure from a slushy runway.

The final three accidents in this group followed failure to: (1) remove one–quarter inch of encrusted snow from the wings; (2) dry the brakes out after taxiing through snow banks; (3) lean the mixtures before takeoff at a high–elevation airport.

CAUSE AND CIRCUMSTANCE

• *Takeoff*

——This phase is composed of the roll and climb through gear and flap retraction. Although this occupies only one percent of the typical business flight, 13 percent of the total number of accidents occurred in this phase of flight.

Of the 12 accidents in this group, two were the result of engine failures, one was caused by bird ingestion (double flameout), and the reason for the other was not determined.

Six of the 12 resulted from loss of control on the takeoff run. Obviously, a basic skill was lacking here. Two other pilots tried to take off from inadequate, unimproved runways; another pilot retracted the gear too soon. The twelfth pilot took off in 100– and–one–half weather conditions the day after his type–rating ride in a jet and lost control of it just after liftoff.

• *Climb*

——The single accident in this phase began with a left engine failure, so perhaps it should be added to the maintenance/service group. But the ultimate cause was loss of control. The airplane spun out of an overcast. Obviously the pilot was lacking in engine–out skills. He had more than 8000 total hours; 27 in type.

• *Cruise*

——Eight accidents are charged to this phase and as you might guess, two of them resulted from attempting visual flight in instrument conditions (both pilots were instrument rated), and two others from fuel exhaustion. In the cruise phase there was one accident each, due to: (1) penetrating a thunderstorm (single engine, no radar); (2) a collision; (3) undetermined; and (4) a fluctuating tach.

138

SELECTIONS

• *En–route Descent*

——The single accident in this phase resulted from a loss of control during letdown with ice.

• *Final Descent*

——This is the phase of flight that's really killing us—both figuratively and actually. If the professionals who fly corporate and business aircraft would concentrate all their skills, knowledge, intuition, and simple attention to these three minutes of the flight, the accident rate could drop 27 percent. More important, 19 lives could have been saved in this one year alone.

Of the 25 accidents that occurred or originated during this phase of flight in 1973, 10 happened during instrument approaches. Five pilots busted minimums. The knowledge they lacked is that busting minimums will kill you; all five pilots died. Radio failure inside the marker caused another fatal IFR accident. Circling under below–circling minimums also resulted in a fatal accident. An improper procedure got another planeful in the mountains near Palm Springs. One pilot saw lights on a night IFR approach, ducked under, and flew into the ground. The lights were from a house, not the runway. The final IFR accident was the result of diving at the final approach glide path so hard that the wings and tail came off.

Downwind landings, failure to lower the gear, and attempts to land on runways that were too short caused three accidents each. Two others were the result of buzzing. An undershoot, an overshoot, and a misread altimeter each resulted in an accident. The twenty–fifth accident in this group occurred because the pilot lined up on the edge of a snow–covered runway instead of the middle.

139

CAUSE AND CIRCUMSTANCE

• *Flare, Touchdown*

——There were nine accidents in this phase. Seven were simply hard landings or stalls in the flare. One occurred after an aerosol can rolled under the pilot's feet and he attempted to kick it out of the way while finishing the landing instead of going around. The ninth was caused by ATC: The tower reported only one inch of snow on the runway, but there was enough to collapse the gear.

• *Rollout*

——The rollout after landing got 10 of the pilots included in this study. Three inadvertently retracted the gear, two lost control on rough fields, and two others simply groundlooped. Hydroplaning was a factor in only one accident in this group. One pilot hit a ditch cut across the runway, and another collapsed a gear at a high-speed turnoff.

• *Taxi–in*

——The three accidents in this phase were the usual type. One pilot nicked a hangar with a wing tip, another was hit by a ramp vehicle and the third was taxiing by some men and equipment when a workman ran out in front of him. The pilot missed the workman but hit the equipment.

We can improve our record significantly by studying this trip profile carefully. Notice that 58 percent of the accidents charged to corporate/executive operations originated in only 10 percent of the total flight time—taxi–out and runup, final descent, flare and touchdown, and rollout.

If we would all apply our skills and knowledge to the fullest during those 14 minutes of each flight, we would improve our safety record—and insurance rates—dramatically.

Aviation Safety Reporting System (August 1977)

In May 1975, in response to a recommendation by a DOT task force looking into aviation safety, the FAA instituted a safety incident reporting program that offered immunity from regulatory enforcement action to those filing such reports.

The basic idea was excellent, but it was ridiculous to think that the FAA could both administer the program and enforce its own regulations. After this was pointed out to them in discussions and editorials, the program was turned over to NASA for implementation and administration in August 1975.

In the years since NASA took the plan over, the Aviation Safety Reporting System has earned the confidence of pilots and controllers and is generating volumes of very useful safety information, although the immunity provisions have recently been modified. Before ASRS (the NASA acronym for it), we had to wait for an accident before a dangerous situation or trend came to light. Now NASA publishes a quarterly review of unsafe situations and actions revealed by the program.

No names are given of course, and the various charts and breakouts of data in the document have little *statistical* meaning, because those who file ASRS reports aren't necessarily representative of all pilots and controllers. However, details of what's going on out there, as published in the quarterlies, is extremely helpful—and frightening. Let's look at some examples:

> • The clearance was as filed, maintain 9000, expect Flight Level 200 three minutes after departure. The departure frequency and transponder code also were given. I missed the first portion of the clearance and picked it up as cleared to FL200. I set 20,000 in the altitude alert unit and set the transponder code as the first officer read back the clearance. Again I did not hear the 9000 restriction.
>
> The first officer made the takeoff and I changed to depar-

ture control and reported leaving 1000 and climbing to FL200. The controller said "Roger" and gave us additional climb instructions, which included a heading change at 2500 feet. At about 8000 feet the first officer asked if we had been cleared to 20,000 and I replied, "Yes." At 10,000 feet the controller asked what altitude we had been cleared to and again I responded 20,000. He said we should have been stopped at 9000, then cleared us to FL200 and asked us to expedite through 11,000, which we did.

The first officer later said he had heard the original clearance to 9000, but he thought we had been recleared to FL200 and that he had missed the reclearance.

• I was cleared to taxi to 27R for takeoff. Upon arrival at the departure end of the runway, I noticed a DC–3 waiting for takeoff from the same runway. My aircraft was under control of the ground controller. He stated, "XYZ, use the stub taxiway to get to the runway; the DC–3 probably will be a while running up." This was interpreted to be a clearance to take position for takeoff. Frequently, at smaller airports, tower and ground operations are conducted by the same person on one radio frequency. After entering the runway, we were advised to taxi clear by the tower due to traffic on final for 27R. We cleared safely while the landing traffic was well out on final.

• The aircraft was operating as a nonstop flight from Los Angeles to Atlanta. The trip left Los Angeles at 2200. The weather from Los Angeles to Atlanta was cloudless with unrestricted visibilities for the entire distance.

Cruise to Atlanta was at 37,000 feet. Approaching Atlanta, the center gave us a clearance to the ATL VOR to cross Dalas Intersection at 12,000 feet. The descent had been started on a previous clearance. A few minutes later the clearance was modified to "direct REX VOR to cross the 30 DME arc of ATL VOR at 12,000 feet, maintain 12,000 feet."

The descent seemed to be going well—balanced against

time, distance and rate of descent—and the groundspeed indicated a very strong tailwind. The center called at what we thought was near the 30 DME arc of ATL and wanted to know what our distance was to the ATL VOR and our altitude. At this point it was discovered that both our VOR receivers were tuned to the REX VOR and that neither pilot was covering the ATL VOR to get the 30–mile fix. As a consequence, we wound up over the 30–mile fix of ATL 3000 feet higher than cleared. We admitted this to center at which time they cleared us to ATL approach control and approach worked us in routinely.

The cause of this incident was a lack of crew coordination relative to which receivers would be set to which VOR.

Secondary cause may relate to time of day and the long nonstop flight, flown entirely on autopilot under absolutely ideal weather conditions. Also there was an almost total lack of any other traffic and radio contacts were made only as required to go from one center to another. There was no other traffic in the ATL area when we arrived.

• We were cleared for the arrival with a crossing restriction of 8000 feet, 25 miles out. There was a flight in trail behind us. The center controller started mixing up the numbers and in the confusion both aircraft answered the wrong calls. The numbers of the flights were similar. We were a little high and the controller asked us if we could make the crossing restriction. Aircraft B answered for us. I said we could probably make it, then asked for a turn to help us get down and received no reply. We then put out speed brakes and made the crossing restriction. In the garble of the communications, we had picked up the approach frequency, so we switched over on our own and reported level 8000 feet. This controller evidently expected us.

• I was working the high sector without a tracker. Aircraft A reported in at FL310 with a rerouting request, which I gave him, to maintain FL 310. Aircraft B (similar number) reported in climbing to FL290, requesting 410. He was restricted to 290 because of A. The sector then began to get busy due to inputting A's route change into the computer and another aircraft entering the sector, which I had no information on. Suddenly, Aircraft B asked me the altitude of the aircraft that just passed him. I informed him that A was level at 310. When I looked closer, I observed A was at 290. When I questioned A, he said he had been cleared to FL290. I called my supervisor. After listening to the tapes, it appears that during a busy period Aircraft A requested permission to deviate east of course. I thought Aircraft B was making the request and read back "Aircraft B, deviation approved, maintain 290." Aircraft A copied that clearance and descended.

WEATHER 11

The relatively higher time, more proficient business pilots to whom this book is directed should experience fewer weather accidents than the pilot population at large. But they don't.

Weather Accidents (February 1976)

We tend to think that an instrument rating is an end–all of weather–related accidents. Not so. Each year we're proved wrong when the NTSB releases its study on weather as a cause/factor in general aviation accidents. In a typical year, there are a total of approximately 4500 general aviation accidents, of which 20 to 25 percent are charged off to weather. It will profit us to study the latter carefully.

The NTSB weather study used for this report covers 962 accidents, of which 272 resulted in one or more fatalities. That breaks out to a weather–related accident for each 32,000 hours of accumulated general aviation hours, and a fatal weather–related accident for each 100,000 hours. When weather is a factor in an accident, the chance of fatality goes up dramatically. In the total accident picture, one in 5.9 results in one or more fatalities; when weather is involved, the ratio jumps to one or more fatalities in each 3.5 weather accidents.

Looking at the total 962 accidents, what were the causes?

As you would expect, the greatest cause of weather accidents is continued VFR into IFR conditions. The NTSB lists this as either the primary cause or as an auxiliary cause in 199 accidents. Again, the NTSB doesn't break out how many of those 199 accidents involved IFR–rated pilots, but in culling through the briefs, we discovered these examples:

• An instrument–rated flight instructor, 2130 total hours, attempted VFR flight into Okmulgee, Oklahoma in a light twin at night. Ceiling 1200, visibility less than three. Two fatalities.

• An instrument–rated flight instructor, 6600 total hours, is believed to have been diverting to Greensboro, North Carolina VFR in a four–place single–engine aircraft that struck a ridge. Sky obscured, ceiling zero. Five (note *five*) fatalities.

• An ATP, 6067 total hours, attempted a VFR approach to Meigs Field, Chicago in less than one–mile visibility in a light twin. He descended into the lake 1.5 miles northeast of the airport. One fatality.

There are many reasons, good reasons, why an instrument–rated pilot may decide to continue VFR into marginal weather. The deterioration of ATC's weather services makes it often prudent to go VFR in imbedded thunderstorm conditions. When severe icing is reported aloft, VFR underneath can be the safer way to go. Certain equipment outages make VFR virtually necessary. (Have you tried to enter a high–density terminal area with an inop transponder recently?)

But pilots must remember that *safe* VFR flight in marginal weather requires infinitely more skill than most IFR operations. If the weather begins to go sour, the instrument–rated pilot flying VFR must be prepared to revert to IFR as a way out of a dangerous situation. Too many IFR–rated pilots flying IFR equipped aircraft on a VFR flight plan (or no flight plan at all) will push on into the side of a mountain rather than admit they've goofed and ask for a clearance.

Powerplant and other equipment failures are listed as the cause in weather–related accidents much less often than most people think. Of the 962 accidents in this study, equipment malfunction is listed as a cause in only 37 instances.

An engine, or engine accessory, is shown as the cause, or one of the causes, 27 times in this study. Significantly, only four of those 27 engine malfunctions resulted in fatalities. And a high proportion of IFR flying is single–engine, which should put to rest the old argument that single–engine IFR is unsafe. It's much, much safer than *not* flying IFR when IFR is called for.

Failures of other kinds of equipment are far more critical than engine loss, according to this study. For instance, of four gyro failures recorded, all resulted in or led to a fatal accident. Of two altimeter failures, one was a factor in a fatal weather accident. The one VOR receiver failure recorded was listed as a factor in a fatal accident; however, incapacitation may also have been a cause or factor in that instance.

Icing conditions, which probably cause IFR pilots more concern than any other weather phenomenon, shows up as a *cause* in only three of these 962 weather accidents; only one was fatal. In 34 other instances, 20 of which were fatal, ice is listed as a *factor*.

One dare not say that ice is an overrated danger in IFR flying, and yet these statistics indicate that a decision to attempt VFR underneath to avoid ice aloft must be weighed extremely carefully. It's impossible to tabulate the rates of ice accidents and VFR–underneath accidents versus exposure, but it's certain that continued VFR is a far bigger killer than ice, although a lot of ice flying is conducted by general aviation pilots.

The same situation exists relative to thunderstorms, but to a lesser degree. Although there's a lot of flying nowadays in thun-

147

derstorm situations, thunderstorms were a cause in only 11 accidents and a factor in 80 others covered in this study. But when thunderstorms are a cause or factor, the result is fatal 51.6 percent of the time.

Unfortunately, the NTSB doesn't tell us how many of these thunderstorm–related accidents occurred in VFR operations or how many in IFR situations. In either event, it's clear that we need better real–time information on thunderstorm activity. If we knew enough about the exact location and nature of heavy weather, 45 to 50 fatal accidents resulting from storm turbulence could be prevented each year. On the other side of the coin, no one can guess how many fatalities have resulted from flight beneath cloud to avoid going IFR through an area of potential thunderstorms, or to avoid an area of scattered cells through which ATC may or may not be of assistance.

Finally, weather includes accumulations of snow and ice on runways, and accidents can also result therefrom. Water, ice, slush, and snow on the runway are a cause/factor in about 41 accidents each year. Running off the centerline into soft shoulders is a cause/factor in an additional 17 accidents annually.

The point of all this is that weather is no respecter of ratings. Too many pilots assume that an instrument ticket in their hip pocket puts weather accidents behind them as well. It's not so.

In the Month of December (December 1977)

For most people in every walk of life, December is the transition month. It's a time to wind up the affairs of one year and get ready for the next, to have one last round of holidaying before settling in for the long stretch to summer vacations—and to get ready to become one year older.

For pilots, December is the month when we must finally say so long to those clear, crisp, VFR days of fall and mentally prepare for the wind, ice, and generally miserable flying conditions of winter.

That transition leads to a unique pattern of December accidents. When you study the record over the years, it becomes clear that we never seem to fully prepare mentally for this month.

Darkness, for example: One evening we're flying home and suddenly realize it's going to be dark before we get there, although the ETA is for only 1830. December is the month of transition from mostly daylight to mostly nighttime operations. A tendency among pilots to lack recent experience in night flying shows in the accident record for December.

At 1649 one December evening, for example, a 25,000–hour captain missed a taxiway at JFK and did major damage to a DC–8. At 1925 hours in Detroit a Cessna 182 pilot allowed a passenger to deplane onto a snowy and slippery ramp while the engine was running. A fatality resulted. At Kansas City, 1935 hours, a Twin Beech captain taxied in without S–turning and crunched both his own airplane and a parked Cessna 172 beyond repair. We all know better than to do that. But in December we don't seem to be quite ready for the extended hours of night. We've lost our night wiliness and caution.

The same is true for water in the tanks. December is a month of temperature contrasts. It's damp and warm one day and crisply cold the next. Result—condensation in fuel tanks, breakdowns in tank truck filters, and water in the gas.

Engines run terribly on water. A California Cessna Skymaster pilot discovered that the hard way one December. When he switched to the auxiliary tanks, *both* engines drowned on the water. At Spring Valley, New York, the pilot of a Piper twin came to grief that same December after losing the left engine at 50 feet on takeoff due to water and ice in the fuel system.

Then there's the carburetor ice problem. After a long summer and crisp, clear fall when pilots don't think much about carburetor

149

ice, December comes, and airplanes with icy carburetors begin dribbling out of the sky from one end of the country to the other.

Ice even gets them out in dry Arizona, as an 11–hour student in a Cessna 150 learned one day after Christmas. And it's not just low–time pilots who forget to use the carburetor heat, or who use it improperly. A few days earlier an Illinois Cessna 182 pilot with 713 hours in type bent his airplane badly (but with no damage to himself or his passenger) because he used carburetor heat improperly.

Ice in all its various forms is a troublesome December problem. Every year someone carelessly taxies through the December slush, takes off, then comes to a sudden and embarrassing stop on his next landing due to frozen brakes. In the latest set of December accident briefs released by the NTSB, it was an Ohio pilot.

In Alaska, a veteran bush pilot (1913 hours in type) discovered a new variation. While he was taking off on floats one chilly December day, his prop picked up so much ice the airplane wouldn't climb. He hit a log bridge but neither he nor any of his seven passengers (yes, seven passengers in a Cessna 180) was injured.

We must remember that December is a time of much water and subfreezing temperatures. In January, that water will be frozen on the ramp and taxiways, but in December it is rippling puddles looking for an airplane on which to freeze.

December also seems to be a month in which relatively inexperienced pilots flying relatively sophisticated airplanes get into trouble with weather. These are the classic "Continued VFR into adverse weather" type accidents, but with a twist.

For example, a noninstrument–rated 310 pilot (an instrument rating should be prerequisite to a twin rating) was crossing Colorado on a poor day and eventually got pushed down into the mountains by a 1200–foot ceiling and snowshowers. He continued pushing until he finally glanced off the ground and damaged the aircraft. That persuaded him to give up and land wheels up on a highway.

Another pilot, this one a 22–year–old private with 93 total hours, launched into a December night in Minnesota under a 300–foot ceiling with visibility less than a mile. He quickly decided that was a bad deal and tried to return to the airport. On downwind he lost sight of the runway, then lost all ground reference turning base to final. He then decided that he had a problem and landed off airport with considerable damage to the airplane, but none to himself or his two passengers.

The NTSB makes no mention of drinking alcohol in that particular accident, but December produces many alcohol–related ones, most of which occur between Christmas and New Year's. Drink utterly destroys judgment, especially at a blood level of 111MG percent. One fellow who did have that much must have been an early drinker. He crashed in zero/zero weather at 1000 hours.

Engine failure incidents pop up often in the December records. We suspect that's because pilots are so anxious to get to grandmother's for Christmas or back home for New Year's that they don't always heed the warning signals.

That was obviously the case for a twin pilot who taxied out and did a runup, but noticed that his fuel pressure was unstable. He decided to go anyway; the left engine quit just as he entered the overcast.

Speaking of fluctuations, December is a month for all kinds of bizarre things you may have never seen before to begin showing up in engines. Occasionally a manifold pressure gauge or an oil pressure indicator will appear fine on the ground, but will drop to zero just after takeoff. It gives you a thrill, but it's only moisture freezing in a capillary line to the instrument panel. Pilots who don't know about that sometimes hurt themselves in their anxiety to get back on the ground.

In December the accumulation of moisture in other odd places can also give you problems, as in push/pull controls, the trailing edge of control surfaces and in the pitot–static system.

Those are by no means all the various kinds of accidents that seem to be particular phenomena of December. Fuel exhaustion incidents, for example, seem to be unnaturally high in December —we can't guess why. And so are maintenance accidents, possibly because most private owners try to duck large bills in the last weeks before Christmas. December also seems to bring on the weird accidents. In December 1975, for instance, two pilots stalled and spun in while hunting fox from airplanes.

Pilots just have to be extra careful in December. If darkness or ice doesn't get you, a fox may.

THREE KINDS OF WIND

12

In addition to huffs and puffs from Mother Nature, pilots must be cautious of those man–made demons: jet blast and wake turbulence.

Windy Weather (November 1976)

When deepest winter comes down on us, our thoughts and apprehensions normally turn to airframe ice, poor visibilities and slippery runways.

But what about wind? This is not really a weather problem in the pure sense. Yet, winter is the season for mighty blows, and each year the NTSB piles up a stack of statistics on pilots who were huffed and puffed into a heap.

A whole series of accidents occur on taxi–out for takeoff. For example, one March a 3250–hour commercial pilot was flipped upside down in a Cessna 182 while taxiing out at Edwards Air Force Base. The weather was CAVU, but the wind was 20 knots, gusting to 38. The only clue to what might have happened is the pilot's 35 hours in type. When handled properly, the 182 is a good airplane in wind. Perhaps it's a bit too good for a high–wing machine, because the weight and stability encourage compla-

153

cency, particularly if the pilot has minimum time in high–wing airplanes.

The cure for a wind upset in any small aircraft is very, very simple. While taxiing in a following wind, simply push the aileron and elevator controls to the downwind corner of the cockpit. That is, in a following wind from the right quarter, turn and push the control wheel into the left/forward corner of the cockpit. In a left quartering tailwind, push the wheel into the right corner.

In a headwind situation, hold the elevators up slightly, and try to roll the airplane into the wind with ailerons. The reason for holding the elevator up is to increase the weight on the main gear so the tires don't begin to slide sideways, allowing the aircraft to weathercock. Pushing the elevators down in a headwind would tend to decrease the angle of attack of the wing and thus decrease lift, which is good. But we've seen the up force generated by down elevators lift the mains totally off the ground. That, of course, utterly destroys the lateral stability of a taxiing airplane and causes a loss of directional control.

Incidentally, takeoff flaps should not be lowered until the airplane is in takeoff position on the runway. You can do without that lift while taxiing into position.

In January of 1975, another Cessna 182 pilot was embarrassed while running a mag check at Portland, Oregon. (I don't mean to pick on the 182—I own one—but they are the most numerous high–wing business aircraft in the fleet, so they turn up in NTSB reports most often.) This pilot evidently was caught in the old right–quartering–tailwind trap.

You've got to think hard about this one. Consider the forces trying to tip an airplane over when it's being runup in *no* wind. First, the rotation of the prop is trying to roll the airplane to the left. Second, the thrust from the prop, acting against locked brakes, is trying to tip the airplane forward. Left roll, tip forward. Since a three–legged airplane has no leg at the forward left cor-

154

ner, the airplane will lean in that direction. Now all you have to do is add a gust from the right rear, and over she goes.

On takeoff, the old left crosswind trick is still doing pilots in with disgusting regularity. The pilot of an Aero Commander 112 who lost it on takeoff from Bellrose, Louisiana one October day is a good example. In a 10–knot left crosswind, gusting to 15, he ran off the runway to the left into a ditch. The cause is clear.

Like every American–built single–engine airplane that pilot had ever flown, the 112 tries to turn left during the takeoff run. His instructor probably told him it was due to torque. Add a left crosswind blowing on the fin and rudder and the left turn tendency is magnified.

In the old tail–dragger days, torque in a left crosswind wasn't much of a problem until you got up into the over–500 hp class. The reason was simple. In a tail–wheel airplane, the steerable tail wheel comes off the ground very soon in a windy day takeoff. Therefore you can begin the takeoff with full rudder deflection if necessary. That gives you maximum aerodynamic help in overcoming the turning forces. As the speed picks up, the rudder is smoothly eased off and the run is straight as a die.

The tricycle gear complicates that. The interconnect between rudder and nosewheel steering makes it impossible to use full rudder deflection. If you try, you end up with too much right nosewheel deflection. So, with the rudder more or less straight, the left wind has more rudder area to push on. That's still okay, as long as the nosewheel is firmly on the ground. But you can leave the nosewheel on the ground only so long.

Try to hold it on with forward stick, and the down elevators will lift the mains off; then the airplane will weathercock, or "wheelbarrow," to the left.

Pull the nosewheel off too soon, and you get another surprise. Since the rudder is hardly deflected, the nosewheel must overcome the left turn tendency induced by torque and the left wind.

Then, as the nosewheel is lifted, the airplane will swing left rather abruptly. Once all that weight up front starts to the left, the momentum—combined with the existing wind force and torque— may prove too much even if the rudder is then jammed hard over. So there you are, nose up, headed for the boonies.

The trick is to lift the nosewheel gingerly and be prepared to add right rudder as it loses traction. If the airplane tries to get away from you, center the rudder pedals (so the nosewheel is straight), then drop the nosewheel back on the ground for positive steering to a higher speed. If nothing seems to work, pull off the power to get rid of the torque, then climb on the brakes and use them for steering. You won't be the first pilot to abort a takeoff in a bad left crosswind situation.

Occasionally some pilot gets himself into trouble with wind en route. A pilot flying an ancient Piper Tripacer near Cape Charles, Virginia collided with the ground on a CAVU day because of turbulence.

Since he was over flat terrain, that had to be the result of inexperience or very poor initial training. In the mountains, however, wind can be a major problem for even the most experienced and skilled pilot. Unless you're an experienced mountain pilot, you would be well advised to stay on the ground when surface winds exceed 15 knots or the winds aloft exceed 25.

Landing accidents due to wind have a dreary sameness to them: The pilot selected the wrong runway, landed downwind; a hard landing due to a wind shift, and the gear collapsed; the pilot lost control after touchdown and hit a snow bank.

The Winter–Weather Accident (October 1976)

In the winter of 1975, a Japan Air Lines captain suffered what must be aviation's greatest embarrassment. Taxiing out for takeoff at Anchorage, Alaska in a 747, he was blown off a taxiway into a ditch. Before you conclude that he must have been dealing with a rip–roaring wind, let us add that the reported velocity was only 20 knots gusting to 33.

Here's what happened, as quoted from the NTSB report:

> The captain stated that he had not experienced any difficulty in taxiing; however, shortly after the tower advisory (relative to ice on the taxiway), the aircraft began to slide to the right. The captain stated that he used both nosewheel steering and brakes to correct the slide, and the aircraft responded satisfactorily, after which he reduced his speed to five knots. He stated that immediately after the correction, the aircraft again began to slide and the nose swung left about 10 degrees to 15 degrees to the taxiway centerline. He applied full brakes and told the first officer to do the same, but the aircraft continued to slide. He applied a small amount of reverse power on all four engines, and the aircraft stopped. He felt that the landing gear was still on the paved surface and that perhaps he had hit a taxiway light. He gave the order to shut down the engines and directed the first officer to call for a tractor to tow the aircraft back. He said that he believed it to be too risky to taxi further.
>
> The aircraft then canted to the right and slowly changed its heading (counterclockwise) to about 70 degrees to the taxiway, slid backward down the embankment and came to rest 90 degrees to the taxiway.

That's a funny kind of accident, but not one any of us can afford to laugh long at, because it wasn't a rare occurrence. Several years ago a friend—then a brand–new American Airlines captain —landed a 707 at Oklahoma City late one windy night in freezing drizzle. He stopped nicely on the runway, but as he started taxiing cautiously up an inclined taxiway to the terminal ramp, the airplane began to slide sidewise. He shut down and sat helplessly as the 707 was blown off the pavement and sank two feet into mud.

157

His 125 passengers had to be evacuated four at a time in a highway patrol car, the only airport vehicle available that miserable night.

Each winter dozens of aircraft are destroyed or severely damaged in silly accidents like these. Because ice on the runway or ramp doesn't degrade an aircraft's motive power the way it does that of a car, we tend to forget that it can totally negate our attempts to stop or steer. We taxi too fast, forget how to use the flight controls to assist in ground steering and attempt to taxi on surfaces we'd avoid in a car.

But as unnecessary and depressing as those accidents are, the ones that occur on takeoffs and landings on snowy and icy runways cause the greatest loss.

Every winter you can be certain that a dozen pilots will misjudge the depth of snow on a runway. The classic case occurred several winters ago when an unwise Aztec pilot from down south arrived over a small Canadian airport for landing. Noting a couple of Cessnas setting high off the snow, he concluded that it was only three or four inches deep.

After they dug him out of the six–foot drifts he had attempted to land on, it was explained to him that the Cessnas were actually setting high up on amphibious floats.

You get the picture. To prevent typical winter accidents, it will help to review some winter dos and don'ts.

• Do make certain the airplane is free of frost, ice, and slush before cranking up. This should be basic to every airman, but accidents continue to happen because pilots try to take off carrying a load of ice. The insidious thing is that what you can get away with once, or even a dozen times, may trap you the next time out.

How often, for example, have you pulled an airplane into a hangar for 10 minutes, knocked the ice off it, then departed without incident? Dozens of times, no doubt.

The last time I tried it, I pulled the airplane out, cranked the

158

engine up and it almost shook itself out of the mounts. The problem was that water had gotten into the spinner and frozen on one side, creating a massive out–of–balance condition.

I was lucky. Another fellow lost an aileron on approach after knocking the visible ice off. In his case, water had frozen inside the trailing edge of the surface. In his high–speed letdown, the out–of–balance situation developed into a near–disastrous flutter.

• Do check out the destination airport carefully before departure. It's not fun to arrive overhead and find the runway hasn't been plowed and the Unicom is out of service. You should start the check–out process by asking Flight Service for NOTAMs. If the destination has a tower, telephone the watch supervisor and ask about the runways *and* taxiways. That JAL captain discussed above got into trouble because airport personnel had not cleared the critical taxiway. You can avoid that condition by knowing precisely what the snow and ice removal situation is before departure.

• Don't assume anything when landing on an icy runway. Last winter a pilot lost a nose gear on a partially cleared runway. When he arrived overhead and saw parts of the runway clear with no vehicles still at work, he assumed the patches of snow left on it were insignificant. Actually, the plow had broken down in the middle of scraping off 10 inches of ice and snow and had been towed in for a quick repair.

• Don't run up on large patches of ice. For starters, you will probably slide 30 feet before you can get the mags checked. A greater danger, however, is that the weight of your nosewheel may break the ice. If that's followed with a runup, the slipstream from your prop could lift a large sheet of ice into the prop arc which could cost you a propeller or even an engine overhaul. It has happened more than once.

In this regard, be especially cautious when taxiing down or crosswind on "rotten" ice. If your wheels break it up, a sheet can

159

be tipped up and forward by the following wind into a prop arc. When taxiing downwind in a prop aircraft, use as much power as is safe to assist in blowing chunks of ice rearward.

• Do be careful about where your tail is pointed when running up. You jet pilots can lift a lot of ice into the engines of the folks behind you when you run the power up just to taxi. This admonition must, of course, be followed by another: Allow more room between you and the airplane ahead of you when you are moving on ice. You'll need it for stopping, and you also must allow for the debris he kicks up.

• Don't land *beside* the runway you had intended to land *on*. That may seem ridiculous, but each winter someone sees a row of runway markers or lights, assumes the other row is under a drift, and lands beside the actual runway or on a taxiway.

• Finally, do be courteous. Give other taxiing aircraft lots of room. Make certain that line personnel aren't treading the slippery ice behind you before you run the power up.

Let's have safer winters. Your insurance man—and mine—begins to think about raising the premiums when he gets called out on a snowy night to look at crumpled wing tips.

Caution, the Jet Blast (October 1974)

A few months ago, there was a humorous story going the rounds about a DC–9 captain who blasted away from the crowded ramp at a smallish airport, rolled a few feet, then stopped before entering the taxiway to allow another aircraft to pass. As he waited, a middle–aged lady charged up and began savagely beating on the nose of his airplane with remnants of the door from her little aircraft.

When he opened a side window to see what the problem was, the lady proved herself no lady, with a short and noisy discourse on the quality of his ancestry, his incestuous sex habits and a

160

rather painful thing he could do with his DC–9.

It developed that the woman had been standing at the nose of her aircraft on the ramp next to the terminal building doing a preflight when the captain fired up. As he swung around to depart, his jet blast struck the open door of her machine and ripped it off its hinges. The door whipped around and smacked her smartly on the backside before rattling across the ramp on the kerosine wind.

She was, of course, somewhat filled with ire by the episode.

Whether or not the story is true, it illustrates a hazard we all too often overlook—jet blast. In the course of a year, several thousand dollars in damage is done to aircraft as the result of a thoughtless moment, and it's not all done by the big jets—or the little ones either for that matter. The other day we watched a Bonanza being run up tail–to–tail with a Turbo Commander. Each time the Bonanza's power went up, the Commander's ailerons were banged brutally against the stops.

On occasion, that sort of thing leads to a nasty accident. In a special study on jet blast hazards, the NTSB reported the crash of a de Havilland Twin Otter on takeoff due to a separated push rod in the elevator control system. Fortunately, no one was killed. Subsequent investigation disclosed that the aircraft had been parked on the ramp for an hour with its tail pointed toward a terminal from which large jets were operating. The crew had failed to perform a proper preflight.

Accidents like that need not happen if we'll all tuck four rules into the back of our heads for recall during appropriate phases of every flight.

First, always inspect the aircraft carefully for jet blast and prop–wash damage before each flight. If the controls were left unlocked after the last flight, even though the airplane was on the ramp only a few minutes, this may involve pulling down some inspection plates to look for structural damage due to control surfaces whipping to their stops.

161

CAUSE AND CIRCUMSTANCE

Second, always know what's behind you before applying breakaway thrust on the ramp or run–up power at the pad. Failure to do so has resulted in spectators being peppered with gravel, mechanics being blown off work stands and windows being shattered in airport lounges and restaurants. Don't be an inconsiderate clod.

Third, refuse takeoffs on runways across which a jet blast or prop wash may be directed. I once very nearly lost control of an aircraft while taking off on Washington National's Runway 3 across the jet blast of a 727 that was holding for a Runway 36 departure at the tail of a line on Taxiway Charlie. Evidently the 727 crew decided to move up, in spite of the tower's call for idle power, just as I passed behind him.

Four years ago a 707 crashed and burned as the result of passing through the jet blast of a DC–9 stuck in mud beside the active runway. The force of the blast was so severe, the 707 crew thought they'd collided with the DC–9. Consequently they attempted an abort with insufficient runway remaining.

Fourth, always put the gust locks in place either before leaving the flight deck or instantly after exiting the aircraft (depending on the type of gust lock employed) at the end of each and every flight. I've become an old maid about this since discovering a cracked aileron spar on my airplane after parking it on a busy ramp just long enough to carry a bag into the waiting room.

If nothing else, attention to these little details will help keep irate women pilots off airport ramps and that in itself will eliminate a significant aviation hazard.

The Wake Upset (October 1972)

Last spring a DC–9 crew swung in behind an arriving DC–10 at Greater Southwest Airport between Dallas and Fort Worth and ended up in a ball of flames scattered down the runway. Why?

162

Wake turbulence—the big curling wind left behind it by every aircraft in flight—has been the subject of hundreds of safety articles over the past 10 years. Yet there are still professional pilots who haven't gotten the word. Some years ago I was being vectored for a visual to Dallas' Love Field, Runway 31 Right, behind a Merlin II. The famous Dallas "Noon Balloon" was in progress, so we were being asked to keep it in tight to cut time between landings to a minimum, and the crew of the Merlin was doing an outstanding job of it. As the 707 captain in front of them came back on his reversers, the Merlin was crossing the Coke plant, so you know how close in and low it was. Just after I had lined up a quarter mile behind it, the Merlin suddenly rolled left about 45 degrees and turned left 20 degrees. It looked like finish for certain, but the crew got it rolled back, lined up, and sat it down. Then a shaky voice came on the frequency and said to no one in particular, "We hit his prop wash."

It wasn't prop wash from a 707, of course. It was a horizontal tornado. Wake vortices are getting bigger and nastier all the time as air carrier aircraft become larger and heavier. Pilots of larger airplanes think wake turbulence is something that only affects guys in Cessnas and Pipers, but that's not so. As that DC–9 crew discovered, you just don't get big enough to stop being cautious about wake turbulence unless you're flying a C–5A or a 747, and it appears that even they are not home free.

The tragedy is that wake–turbulence accidents are totally unnecessary. There is still a great gray area in our knowledge of wake turbulence, but this much is certain: The vortices form off the wing tips of every airplane, large or small. The heavier the generating aircraft the greater the intensity of these vortices. A few years ago it was thought that the two vortices drifted downward and outward. Recent investigation has shown, however, that they drift together a few feet, then sink side by side at 400 to 500 fpm down to 800 or 900 feet below the generating aircraft's flight path. If the ground intervenes, they drift apart at about five knots.

The drift rate and direction are affected by crosswinds, and allowances must be made for that. There is no evidence that the vortex itself will rise under any conditions, but there is an unofficial belief that at higher elevations, the residual chop will rise on a gentle updraft.

Since the movement of wake turbulence relative to the generating aircraft is highly predictable, you don't really need to know much about wakes to avoid having a problem: All you have to do is stay above the flight path of the wake maker. That isn't hard to do if you use your head. Since the heavies do not lay down a wake unless they are generating lift, you can take off behind them with no fear so long as you lift off shorter than they did, and either climb as steeply as they did or turn out before crossing through their flight path. When taking off behind a landing heavy, note

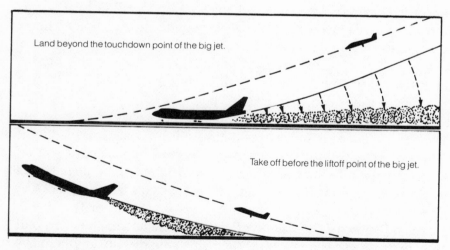

Land beyond the touchdown point of the big jet.

Take off before the liftoff point of the big jet.

(October 1972)

where his nose gear touched down and do not lift off before that point. Do not accept intersection takeoffs—ever—and be super-cautious when using an intersecting or parallel runway.

When landing, always plan to land well beyond the touchdown zone of the heavies. Some pilots brag that even on 10,000–foot runways, they try for the numbers on every landing—so they'll be sharp when they have to go into a short field. That's not very smart. Spot–landing practice is good, but pick a spot 2000 feet from the end of the runway, because the heavies aim for 1000 feet. Land long and live longer.

If pilots will remember the simple rule—STAY ABOVE THE FLIGHT PATH OF THE WAKE MAKER—this kind of accident will become extinct.

THE STALL SPIN

13

Next time a pilot friend bids you goodbye with the admonition, "Keep Your Nose Down," take it as the sincerest form of wishing you long life.

The Stall Spin (March 1973)

The National Transportation Safety Board some years ago issued a special study on the stall/spin accident records of 37 selected aircraft types. Of 991 accidents studied, 43.1 percent resulted in fatalities, so this is an accident cause with a circumstance that should command our attention.

As one would expect, business and corporate aviation does not figure prominently in the study; only 76 of the 991 stall/spin accidents covered are assigned to business aviation operations. Another four are charged to corporate aircraft flown by professional crews. That only 80 stall/spin accidents were charged to business aviation—8.07 percent of the total—seems laudable until one looks at the records of other groups. Pleasure pilots, of course, have by far the worst record; 491 or 49.55 percent of the total. Various training and practice activities are next, with 214 accidents for 21.59 percent, followed by ag operations with 105 accidents and 10.59 percent.

166

But look at this. Air taxi operators, who have often been casti-gated by the CAB for their safety record, accounted for only 18 of the 991 accidents covered in this study—only 1.82 percent against the 8.07 percent for business and corporate operators. Obviously business flyers need to take a closer look at their in-volvement in this kind of safety hazard.

First, in what kind of airplanes do business and corporate pilots have stall/spin accidents? For corporate pilots they occurred, one each, in a Beech Baron, a Piper Comanche, a Twin Comanche and (yes) a Super Cub.

For businessmen pilots the record in twins was:

Beech 95/95–55 (Baron or Travelair) _ _ _ _ _ _ _ _ _ 4
Piper 23 series (Apache and Aztec) _ _ _ _ _ _ _ _ _ _ 4
Cessna 310 _ 3
Cessna Skymaster_ _ _ _ _ _ _ _ _ _ _ _ _ _ _ _ _ _ 1
Piper Twin Comanche _ _ _ _ _ _ _ _ _ _ _ _ _ _ _ _ 1

For businessmen flying singles:

Mooney_ 9
Bonanza/Debonair_ _ _ _ _ _ _ _ _ _ _ _ _ _ _ _ _ _ 7
Tripacer _ 6
Cessna 182 _ 5
Cessna 150 _ 4
Piper Cub _ 4
Beech Musketeer _ _ _ _ _ _ _ _ _ _ _ _ _ _ _ _ _ _ 3
Cessna Cardinal_ _ _ _ _ _ _ _ _ _ _ _ _ _ _ _ _ _ _ 3
Piper Cherokee _ _ _ _ _ _ _ _ _ _ _ _ _ _ _ _ _ _ _ 3
Super Cub _ 3
Cessna 120/140 _ _ _ _ _ _ _ _ _ _ _ _ _ _ _ _ _ _ _ 2
Cessna 172 _ 2
Luscombe _ 2

167

The other eight stall/spin accidents charged to business aviation occurred, one each, in an Aeronca Champ, Aeronca Sedan, Cessna 175, Cessna 180, Cessna 210, Forney Ercoupe, Piper Super Cruiser, and Piper Pawnee agplane.

The above is by no means a rating. It doesn't relate to how many hours each aircraft type is flown on business, so exposure isn't taken into account. The NTSB did, however, look at some of the airplanes from the standpoint of total hours flown for pleasure, practice *and* business and then rated them using the chi-square statistical method. Here's what they found:

AIRCRAFT	STALL/SPIN FREQUENCY
Aeronca 11 Series	Very high
Cessna Cardinal	Very high
Piper Super Cub	Very high
Stinson 108 Series	High
Beech Baron/Travelair	High
Cessna 172 Series	Low
Cessna 180 Series	Low
Cessna 206 Series	Low
Piper Comanche	Low
Beech Bonanza/Debonair	Very low
Cessna 182 Series	Very low
Cessna 210 Series	Very low
Piper Cherokee	Very low

Perhaps more important than what kinds of airplanes are involved and to what degree, is what phase of flight has proved the most troublesome. Again, the NTSB does not do a breakdown for business pilots only, but it does for the combined operations. Not surprisingly, buzzing, low passes, aerobatics, and ag operations account for the highest percentage.

The next most prevalent phase involved was approach and landing: 358 accidents. Looking at approach and landing stall/

spin accidents in the aircraft types most often flown by business-men, there are 16 in twins and 30 in high–performance singles.

Improper executions of go–arounds resulted in 73 of these landing phase stall/spin accidents. There's no excuse for that. Interestingly, not all go–around mishaps were in old, underpowered, slippery airplanes. Two occurred in Cessna 310s, two in Bonanzas, one in a Baron, five in Piper Cherokees.

The takeoff phase yielded 238 stall/spin accidents. Again, not all of them were in nonsense–type airplanes; one occurred in an Aero Commander twin, two in Beech 18s, two in Cessna 206s, seven in Comanches.

The question arising out of this mass of data (the NTSB study, including an appendix, runs to 110 pages) is what are we doing wrong and what can we do to cut down on the frequency of stall/spin accidents?

The NTSB made five broad suggestions to the FAA, in the hope of causing a reduction in stall/spin accidents:

(1) Anti–stall/spin training, including reinstitution of spin recovery practice (which was removed several years ago from the requirements for private and commercial pilots).

(2) Evaluation of more sophisticated anti–stall devices—such as stick shakers, stick pullers and angle–of–attack indicators—for use on smaller aircraft.

(3) Increased awareness of the problem through advisory circulars, bulletins from pilot organizations, and magazine articles giving special emphasis "to the potential occurrence of [stall/spins] as a result of improper operation of powerplant or powerplant controls, inadequate preflight preparation and/or planning, mismanagement of fuel and other causes characteristically attributed to the pilot."

Furthermore, the NTSB says, "Maintenance personnel should also be advised of the history of stall/spin accidents precipitated by engine failure or malfunction due to inadequate maintenance and inspection."

(4) Raise the minimum altitude to 500 feet everywhere.

(5) Careful study of the problem by the FAA, NASA and the National Aerial Applicators Association directed towards development of improved anti–stall/spin training and of stall/spin resistant aircraft.

Since that report was issued, NASA has been hard at work developing a spin resistant aircraft, and airframe manufacturers are also looking harder at the problem.

Until these efforts bear fruit, the rest of us need to keep reminding ourselves that the stall/spin is a maneuver very injurious to health. In its study, the NTSB found that the stall/spin accounts for only eight percent of the total accidents but is the direct cause of 22 percent of the deaths in general aviation.

So, next time a pilot friend bids you goodbye with the admonition, "Keep your nose down," take it as the sincerest form of wishing you long life. He's telling you how avoid one of the biggest killers in aviation.

The V$_{MC}$ Accident (September 1976)

In early August of 1976 the engine–out accident received national prominence when Congressman Jerry Litton and his family were killed in the crash of a light twin on departure from Chillicothe, Missouri. The accident drew national attention, including a story in *Time* magazine. Representative Litton was going to a celebration of his victory in the Missouri primary for U.S. Senator when the accident occurred. His wife and two children were onboard and the plane was being flown by a friend, who was accompanied by his son.

The NTSB quickly indicated that a primary factor in the accident was failure of the left engine just after liftoff due to a broken crankshaft. But is that *really* a cause for a fatal accident in a light twin?

The answer is emphatically *no*. The reason why people are killed after an engine failure on departure in a light twin is very, very simple: They try to continue flight, get too slow, and consequently spin in.

Many wise twin pilots say, only half facetiously, that twins should be rigged so that when one engine fails at any altitude below 500 feet agl, the other one will automatically fail. As silly as that may seem, the NTSB statistics clearly indicate that such a measure would result in fewer fatal twin accidents.

In 1972 the Board released a Special Study on engine–failure–related accidents for the years 1965 through 1969. During that period there were 455 accidents due to an engine malfunction or failure in a twin. Deaths resulted in 104 (22.9 percent) of those accidents.

In that same period, there were 3855 engine–failure–related accidents in single–engine aircraft. Deaths resulted in 208 of them, *or in only 5.4 percent.*

Furthermore, looking at the fatal accident *rate* in engine–failure–related accidents for twins in those years, it was 0.516 per 100,000 hours; *for singles it was only 0.247.*

Let's put that another way so you don't miss it. Statistically speaking, you can expect to fly a single–engine airplane 405,005 hours before being killed due to an engine failure; in a twin you can expect *less than half that*, 193,946 hours, to be precise— according to those NTSB records.

Although that picture has undoubtedly changed in the years since the NTSB's study, due to better designed twins and improved pilot proficiency, it's obvious there is something about the small twin–engine airplane that makes it *twice* as susceptible to an engine–failure fatal accident as an airplane with only one engine.

Everyone knows precisely what it is. It's asymmetrical thrust. With one engine windmilling and the other at full power, it takes a lot of opposite rudder and aileron to keep the wings level. All of that creates enormous drag, and if the airspeed is allowed to get too low, the controls lose effectiveness, the airplane will do a slow roll and the people in it will be killed. There's no less macabre way to say it; let the airplane get too slow, and there are going to be pieces of bodies all over the cornfield.

Aviation safety experts, twin manufacturers, insurance underwriters, magazine writers and editors, instructors, and accident investigators agonize in frustration because so many pilots of twins cannot be made to believe that.

For years we have preached V_{MC}—velocity of minimum control. Now we've begun to hear a new V speed discussed, V_{SSE}, which is an acronym for the minimum velocity for safe single–engine flight. Beech Aircraft engineers seem to have coined the acronym (although Cessna has shown a "recommended safe single–engine speed" in its twin manuals for years), and they are pushing hard for its adoption by all twin manufacturers. We heartily endorse that movement.

But we're not convinced that a stated limiting speed is the answer to the basic problem. To get a twin rating, every pilot must have a knowledge of, and demonstrate a familiarity with V_{MC}. Still, far too often when an engine fails they allow the speed to bleed off to a sub–V_{MC} value and then freeze on the throttles as the airplane rolls onto its back and plows into the ground.

The reason, of course, is panic. Somehow, twin pilots must be conditioned not to panic when an engine fails. On the theory that such preparation can best be accomplished by spreading knowledge, let's review the three major light–twin facts of life.

• *Twins don't fly well on one engine*

——When they move into twins, most pilots put the prospect of a forced landing totally out of their minds. That's a major mistake. When an engine quits at a critical point in the takeoff, or on a go–around, the possibility of achieving climb in a light piston twin, or of even maintaining level flight is slim. In fact, the possibility is nil unless all the conditions are perfect. For that reason, on every takeoff and every arrival the light–twin pilot must think just like his single–engine counterpart—where can the airplane be landed in the event of an engine failure. If the pilot hasn't picked his spot beforehand, when the engine does quit, he has no alternative except to sit with his right arm stiff on the throttles and hope by some miracle that the airplane will climb. If it doesn't, panic is guaranteed.

• *Speed control has precedence over everything else*

——Light–twin pilots must understand that after an engine failure, nothing is more important than maintaining the proper speed. Most instructors teach, and most engine–failure checklists indicate, that configuring the airplane for one–engine climb is paramount. Actually, getting the props, power, gear and flaps up, and the engine feathered, becomes academic if in the process of doing so the airplane rolls inverted five feet off the runway. Remember, when an engine quits, the *primary* thing between you and death is V_{SSE}. Grab hold of it and hang on for dear life. *After* you've saved your life, give a little thought to saving the airplane by cleaning it up and establishing best rate–of–climb speed (which really means least rate–of–descent speed).

• *Power becomes an alternative control with an engine out*

——If all fails and you do get too slow, the resulting roll can be controlled by *reducing power* on the operating engine. If the airplane begins to get away from you, pull the throttles back. Don't think that getting the bad engine feathered or the gear and flaps up will save the situation. Once that roll begins, nothing will save your life except a reduction in power.

That's a very, very difficult thing to accept. Every fiber in you wants *more* power. Your intuition tells you that more power will prevent a crash into the trees at the end of the runway. But remember, it's better to hit the trees wings level than to hit the ground inverted.

Let's say it one final time: Don't let the V_{MC} accident be your end—*watch your airspeed.*

THE MIDAIR 14

After each collision between an air carrier
and a general aviation aircraft, the pressure
grows to ban little airplanes from airspace
used by airliners. The most recent was at
San Diego in September 1978. The tragedy
is that if the pilots of the two aircraft
involved had read the following reports of
earlier collisions, San Diego need not have
been.

Midair Collisions (January 1976)

In January 1975, a Twin Otter commuter and a Cessna 150 collided over Whittier, California. The 12 persons onboard the Twin
Otter (two crew and 10 passengers), and the student pilot and
instructor in the 150 were killed.

This accident was a typical collision: It occurred in the vicinity
of an airport—Los Angeles International; the aircraft approached
one another outside the normal traffic scan areas of the crews; and
at least one of the crews was being given radar traffic advisories
at the time. Despite the fact that the details make for a familiar
old story, this particular accident has something important to
teach us.

CAUSE AND CIRCUMSTANCE

It occurred at 1607 hours, local time, as the Twin Otter was proceeding west, into the sun, for a landing at LAX. The weather was high, thin overcast; visibility, 40 miles. The Otter crew had contacted LAX approach control approximately three minutes before the impact, and the aircraft's transponder return and altitude readout were acquired by the LAX ARTS III equipment and verified by the controller.

Approximately two minutes before impact, the approach controller informed the Otter crew they had traffic, a police helicopter, at 12 o'clock, 5.5 nm, climbing from 1500 to 3000 feet. At that time the Otter was descending through 2600 feet. The controller said he would "point him (the helicopter) out again when he's a little closer. . . ."

Meanwhile, the Cessna had departed Long Beach airport approximately 21 minutes prior to the collision. It was occupied by a student pilot taking a final check prior to examination for a private license, and a 47–year–old, 22,000–hour flight instructor who had many years experience in the Los Angeles area. The Cessna evidently proceeded north at about 2200 feet outside TCA airspace towards the El Monte Airport. There were no radio communications with the Cessna crew after it departed Long Beach, nor was the aircraft equipped with a transponder.

Because it was proceeding on a tangential track relative to the LAX radar, a primary return was probably not displayed to the controller. Subsequent tests with another Cessna 150 disclosed that a non–transponder–equipped aircraft flying the course and altitude of the hapless Cessna would not be tracked by the radar in use at the time of the accident.

Studies have shown that a pilot's normal traffic scan is 45 degrees to either side of 12 o'clock. A plot of this collision indicates that the Otter came in on the Cessna at approximately 57 degrees right of 12 o'clock, descending from right to left. The Otter, therefore, would have been masked by the Cessna's right wing.

176

The plot also indicates that the Cessna came in on the Otter at approximately 33 degrees left of 12 o'clock. The rate of closure was 174 knots, or 284 feet per second. Relative to the Otter, the Cessna would have been to the left of directly into the sun.

The key to the cause of this accident is the traffic report given to the Otter crew just before impact. The NTSB sums it up nicely:

> About one minute 15 seconds before the collision, the controller advised GLW 261 of helicopter traffic directly in front of them and climbing past the altitudes through which they were descending. The controller also told them he would point out the traffic again when it was closer, and asked them to let him know when they had it in sight. The next advisory from the controller did not occur until after the collision. There can be no doubt that an advisory of traffic directly in front of them and climbing through their altitude would have commanded the flight crew's attention. An advisory of this nature constituted such a clear and apparent threat to their safety that the pilots could be expected to *channel their visual scan to a narrow sector directly in front* of their aircraft until the traffic had been acquired visually, until they were informed the traffic was no longer a factor, or until they were satisfied that a sufficient time interval had passed to insure that they had passed the traffic. They knew that the first two eventualities had not occurred, and it does not seem logical to infer that they assumed the latter eventuality had occurred. The Safety Board believes that the pilots of GLW 261 had limited their visual search in an area to acquire a known target that constituted a definite threat, and therefore either did not see the Cessna, or did not see it in sufficient time to institute timely evasive action.

The emphasis is ours, and there's the chief lesson to be learned from this accident. We've seen it happen time and again. ATC calls out traffic at one o'clock, six miles, and everyone in the airplane leans forward and begins to search the one o'clock sector.

When you analyze it, that's illogical. If you're below 10,000 feet, the closure interval on traffic at six miles will be a minimum of 43 seconds, even if you're both indicating the maximum allowable 250 knots. Odds are heavy that the interval will be more like 75 seconds, minimum. That's because most aircraft capable of maintaining 250 knots in a terminal area are in contact with ATC, and so won't be called as bogy traffic. You'll be given the aircraft type, its altitude, anticipated changes in altitude and its direction of flight. Therefore, it's not the fast traffic you normally need to be concerned about, and if you use logic, you'll know how much time you have before slow traffic becomes a panic.

In the case of the Otter crew, a callout of helicopter traffic at 5.5 miles climbing should have told them they had at least one minute before there would be a threat from this *known* traffic. That one minute should have been used in searching for *unknowns*.

In our cockpit, we've conditioned ourselves to do just that. When traffic is called, we take that as a reminder to look all around, to make sure no one is sneaking in on us, before beginning to concentrate on the indicated sector. It's amazing how often that pre–concentration search turns up a bogy.

The next consideration is what you do about the traffic once it's visually acquired. Again, time after time, we've seen pilots become mesmerized by another airplane in relatively close proximity. We dropped that habit long ago after spotting an opposite-direction F–105 going by on the right, but failing to see his buddy until he flashed by on the left. Since then, we assume that where there's one airplane, there must be two. As soon as spotted traffic is assessed as no immediate threat, we quickly look around for his buddy. If there are two pilots onboard, the spotted traffic is assigned to the copilot for continued surveillance, which frees the captain to look for others.

178

While you don't want to be mesmerized by known traffic, neither do you want to become so absorbed in looking elsewhere that you forget to continually update your assessment of the known danger.

Lest we seem to be placing all the blame for this accident on the Twin Otter crew, let us also evaluate the actions of the student and instructor in that Cessna. Both should have been aware that the training situation calls for extra vigilance. By definition, training suggests preoccupation: The instructor talks and the student listens. The wise instructor looks while he talks, and instills in his student a habit of looking while he listens.

More important, every pilot who has elected to eschew ATC services in a terminal area should be thoroughly familiar with the inbound and outbound routes. There are those who will argue that this instructor shouldn't have been where he was without a transponder; or at the very least, he should have contacted approach before flying through the low–level paths to and from the Los Angeles basin and LAX.

But without knowing the local VFR–versus–ATC situation, that would be an unfair prejudgment. Maybe LAX controllers haven't the inclination to work VFR traffic in that area, so old–timers have ceased calling them.

A situation like that exists in the area west of New York, and we've learned to cope with it by being especially vigilant when crossing the known paths of low–level inbounds to La Guardia, Newark, and Teterboro. Had this instructor raised a wing now and then to look for inbounds descending on him from the east into LAX, he almost certainly would have spotted the Otter in that 40–mile visibility in time to avoid it.

All this leads to a discourse on professionalism. In regard to the collision threat, professionalism demands three things:

• *A collision–avoidance routine*

——Each crewmember should develop well thought–out scan habits. Condition yourself to scan at least 120 degrees each time something reminds you of the collision threat. Examples of reminders are a traffic callout from ATC, each sighting of an aircraft, and each change in altitude or attitude. The scan should be purposefully more than 45 degrees to either side of 12 o'clock. Lean forward and look around cockpit obstructions. Keep the head moving as well as the eyes. Don't forget to look up and down. Turn on all your exterior lights.

• *Rules of thumb for estimating time to an ATC–provided target*

——In the airplane we fly most of the time, we assume we have a minimum of 12 seconds for each mile of separation from opposite–direction traffic; 24 seconds for crossing traffic. With that knowledge, we know that if we don't see one–mile traffic on first glance, it's either no factor or too late. At four miles, we know we have time to take a quick look, sweep other areas for unreported traffic, then go back to the indicated sector for a thorough search.

• *Awareness of where the bogies are most likely to pop up*

——Obviously, one should always be wary when approaching a VOR, crossing an ILS or cutting through the extension of a runway. In addition, the professional makes it his business to know about local peculiarities. In the New York area, for example, we've learned that low–level traffic tends to follow the Hudson; that in poor visibility commuters use the White Plains outer compass locator for sneaking across from Newark to New Haven; that the Jersey shoreline is a flyway for Sunday pilots.

180

Some day we're going to have onboard electronic assistance in spotting traffic. Meantime, the professional approach can be a very effective collision–avoidance system—provided it's applied with creativity and intellect.

Collision Avoidance (May 1973)

Following every midair collision the FAA will predictably issue another brief giving its views on collision–avoidance systems. Although CAS has seldom been in the news recently, it is an exceedingly hot potato in Washington. Everyone is aware of the possibility that a collision involving a loaded wide–body jet could stampede Congress into demanding, by legislation if necessary, a full–blown CAS.

The gist of the most recent FAA paper is that CAS technology is still so imperfect that even a decision on the kind of system that should be implemented cannot be made before the 1980s. Coincidentally, long before then the FAA hopes to have its own in–house–developed system, called Synchro DABS, in flight test.

Whichever way this hot potato is handed off, it's evident that pilots and crews are going to have to rely on see–and–avoid, plus their wits, for a long time. Wits can be as effective in collision avoidance as the eyes. The technique is simple: Know when to look out, where to look, and what sort of collision threat will most likely be seen—head on, overtaking, or converging.

The FAA has an ongoing collision study based on NTSB records that can give us some valuable clues in applying wits to the problem. For instance, the study shows that at uncontrolled airports only 11 percent of the collisions involve a departing aircraft while 71 percent occur during landings. Obviously, at uncontrolled airports, caution should be exercised during takeoffs, and *super* caution must be exercised during landings. It also helps to know that 80 percent of the collisions at uncontrolled

181

airports occur during the last 275 feet of the descent.

At controlled airports, too, most collisions occur during the landing phase, but here they tend to happen earlier in the approach—about 60 percent after leaving 1000 feet agl but before descending out of 500 feet. In contrast to uncontrolled airports, only 20 percent of the collisions at controlled airports occur below 275 feet.

Notice what this tells you: At uncontrolled airports crews would be well advised to prepare the aircraft for landing and perform other head–down chores early in the approach; at controlled airports, however, just the reverse is true; leave the head-down tasks until the last moment.

Not surprisingly, most airport collisions are due to overtaking or being overtaken. Since business and corporate pilots normally fly higher–performance aircraft, the thing to look out for, therefore, is a slower airplane that you are likely to be overtaking.

En route, collisions occur at altitudes as high as 16,000 feet. Most pilots tend to relax after climbing through 10,000 feet, but actually 15 percent of the risk still lies above 10,000 feet for an IFR aircraft. The greatest en–route collision risk, however (about 70 percent), is below 4000 feet. More fatalities result from en-route collisions, incidentally, than from those occurring in the vicinity of an airport.

Convergence angles in en–route collisions present a baffling picture. If you are VFR the risk versus other VFR aircraft is to overtake or be overtaken. But the risk versus IFR aircraft is head–on.

In the absence of a CAS, pilots should think about all this. A little bit of knowledge added to the basic eyeball can make a big difference.

The Civil/Military Collision (May 1975)

If you've got as much as 500 hours of cross–country time in your log, chances are good that at one time or another you've sat in your cockpit in a blue rage, shouting loudly about the thimble-sized brain of a nearby military pilot.

Near–misses with the military are frequent occurrences—and not all of them are happenstance near–misses. Some are deliberate high–speed passes.

The first time it happened to me, I was at 20,000 feet several miles northeast of Wichita, running performance checks on an early turbocharged Skymaster. My copilot sensed the two F–105s coming in. He suddenly took the controls and lifted the right wing to reveal the pair streaking in from our blind spot just above the wing. One went just under us, the pilot looking up and no doubt grinning through his oxygen mask; the other, just in front of us.

Since then, similar incidents have happened to me many, many times—both deliberate passes by pea–brained GIs and near-misses with military traffic conducting irresponsible operations—and I'm not alone. In response to a magazine article on this subject I received several letters from readers saying they had had similar experiences. One of the more interesting was from Martin Caidin, author of a string of novels and books on aviation.

"Some years ago," Caidin wrote, "flying Debonair 935T (with Jim Yarnell of Beech in the airplane with me), we were doing photography over Nashville, positive control all the way. We always called in, got a good radar track and listened carefully to and obeyed what the people on the ground said. Cloud bottoms were about 6000 feet, and we were rolling out of a turn for a photo pass. We looked up to clear the turn and, lo and behold, there was this very big C–119 dropping out of the clouds on a direct collision course. No word from anyone—except ours after the incident. Radar didn't even know the 119 was there.

"We used to have a problem with Patrick AFB here in Florida, when people were flying C–124B monster Globemasters into Patrick. They had a habit of a long approach to the northeast from over the mainland, and nearly went right through the Melbourne Regional Airport at a perfect 800 feet, in the middle of the pattern traffic. That ended when one enraged doctor rolled out of his violent escape maneuver, followed the C–124B into Patrick and raised absolute hell until he talked with the base commander—who, by the way, agreed with the doctor and put an end to *that* kind of approach."

Hopefully, the military everywhere will prove as cooperative as that base commander at Patrick because the NTSB has recently sent a safety recommendation to the Department of Defense asking them to: "Take positive action to assure that such low–level military intercept operations are confined to designated restricted airspace."

The particular low–level intercept operation the NTSB referred to occurred after dark on the evening of October 11, 1974. An hour or so earlier, Bob Axley had departed White Plains, New York in a 250 Comanche en route to Georgetown, South Carolina with his wife and two children onboard. He had filed a VFR flight plan and was receiving VFR radar advisories from ATC en route.

At 2010:29 Axley was handed off to a Washington Center controller and checked in over Salisbury, Maryland on Victor One, level at 8500 feet. At 2022:12 Center called, saying: "Seven Six Papa, you have traffic in your six o'clock position, five to seven miles, southeast bound, indicating VFR below 10. He's slowly overtaking you."

Axley responded, "Seven Six Papa, we'll be looking over our shoulder here."

At 2023:07 center called again, "Seven Six Papa, he's in your eight o'clock position now and about five miles, and he looks like he's going to be off your left wing."

Seven Six Papa never responded.

Meanwhile, two New Jersey Air National Guard F–106 aircraft were conducting a high–speed (Mach 0.48/311 KTAS) chase down Victor One at about 5000 feet. They weren't in contact with Washington Center; instead they were being worked by the North American Air Defense Command (NORAD) facility at Fort Lee, Virginia. Aircraft EL08 was being vectored for a stern attack at Aircraft EL10. At 2019:42 the NORAD controller told EL10 he had traffic, range eight miles and said, "You should be clear of it." Ten seconds later, almost in the same breath, the NORAD controller gave EL08 a bearing on his target aircraft EL10.

The chase continued in spite of the civil traffic up ahead. At about 2023:11, EL08 struck the Comanche from the rear. The Comanche, parts of its right wing and tail severed, plummeted straight down. EL08, piloted by Captain Michael Kelly, landed intact at NAFEC, Atlantic City.

In its report on the fatalities, the NTSB observed, "The NORAD controller was aware of the conflicting traffic and advised EL08 and EL10 of its location three times. However, neither he nor the pilots suspended the intercept operation. In fact, the NORAD controller cleared EL08 for an attack with the conflicting traffic at 250 degrees, four miles from EL08 and EL10, when actually the F–106s were two miles apart and EL08 was closing within one mile of the conflicting traffic. EL10 acknowledged that he saw the traffic and apparently assessed it as no threat to him. However, EL08 either did not see N6876P or saw it, returned to his intra–cockpit duties and, in maneuvering to salvage the initially aborted run, inadvertently locked on the civil aircraft rather than EL10. This probability is substantiated by the fact that EL08 climbed from the initial intercept altitude of 6000 feet to the collision altitude of 8500 feet—the cruising altitude of the Piper."

The cause of this accident is perfectly clear. The scary thing is that there is so little we civil pilots can do to prevent recurrences.

185

In looking into the background of this accident, I discovered that on November 20, 1967, A. W. League, then the FAA director of air traffic services, gave the Air Force written permission to conduct missions such as those that occurred on the evening of October 11, 1974, with *no provision* to coordinate with ATC or to alert civil aircraft in the area. Thus we can't even file a violation on military aircraft observed breaching FARs.

We can do the following, however:

(1) Notify the FAA of every observed breach of FARs by a military aircraft, so the information can be put into the hands of people with authority to stop it.

(2) For what little it's worth, always work center when in an area where military operations may be in process.

TECHNIQUES   15

As is true of every craft, flying involves the use of established techniques. Some are operational, such as how to execute an ILS approach or land in a crosswind. But the important aviation techniques are those that improve safety.

The "What If" Game (August 1975)

On June 24, 1974, a G–II crashed near Kline, South Carolina. The G–II was on a training flight out of Savannah with two company pilots and a Grumman American instructor onboard. All three were killed.

When the NTSB released its report on the accident, there were no surprises. As had been hinted in some previously released information, the Board determined that the accident was caused by "an unwanted extension of the ground and flight spoilers, which resulted in a loss of control at an altitude from which recovery could not be made."

As a result of its investigations, the Board arrived at these findings:

(1) The only evidence of an aircraft malfunction was the extended position of the ground spoiler panels at impact.

(2) The elevator trim tab position was full nosedown to the

187

electrical trim stop. The aileron manual trim was set 9.5 degrees left wing down.

(3) The landing gear and the wing flaps were retracted at impact.

(4) The right and left ground spoilers were unlocked and extended in flight. Their exact position could not be determined. The inboard and outboard flight spoilers on each wing were extended between 24 degrees and 55 degrees, and 24 degrees and 35 degrees, respectively.

(5) The left ground spoiler panel actuator was fractured, probably by high airloads.

(6) The cause of the unwanted ground spoiler extension was probably a hot electrical short, which bypassed the four ground spoiler interlocks installed in the system.

(7) The extension of the ground spoilers caused the flight spoilers to extend.

(8) This unwanted extension of the spoilers occurred at a relatively low airspeed, and when the aircraft was in a landing approach configuration.

(9) The unwanted extension of the spoilers resulted in an upset and a rapid loss of altitude.

(10) The pilots probably attempted recovery from this upset by retracting the gear and flaps, increasing power, and accelerating the airplane to a speed of more than 300 knots.

(11) The resulting high airloads failed the actuator rod of the left ground spoiler, which resulted in lateral asymmetry and high rolling moments.

(12) During their attempts to recover from the ensuing rolls, the pilots may have inadvertently activated the electric elevator trim tab to the full nose–down position.

(13) The pilots were unable to maintain pitch control and had insufficient altitude in which to recover from the ensuing dive.

One could, as the NTSB did, wrap it up there with recommendations designed to ensure that no future electrical short will cause an inadvertent ground spoiler deployment on a G–II. Looking at the record, however, since this was the first loss of a G–II due to a short around the various spoiler deployment safety devices, that recommendation will probably prevent one accident over the next seven years. We should be able to gain more in safety knowledge from this tragedy than that.

Hints of what the accident should teach us are found in the description of aerodynamic studies the NTSB conducted in order to determine the probable cause. But a better way to get at the events leading up to the crash is to play a game called "What If." Pilots who hope to reach retirement age should play "What If" often. Here's how the game goes.

Pick any system on any airplane—say the ground spoilers on a G–II—and ask yourself, "What if they go berserk and deploy in flight?"

If you know the airplane as you should, you'll be aware that when the ground spoilers go out, the flight spoilers also deploy. Also, there's no annunciator to tell you the ground spoilers are out, and you can't see them from the cockpit, so you'll probably guess that only the flight spoilers deployed. Your natural reaction will be to try to retract them with the normal flight spoiler control. If that fails to bring them down (and with the ground spoilers deployed they can't come down), you'll probably try killing hydraulic pressure with the flight power shutoff valve in an attempt to get them to blow down.

What if all that happened? What would the consequences be? First, of course, when all those boards popped out, the airplane would drop like a brick. If the airspeed were low, the airplane might stall and fall off, momentarily out of control. Your natural reaction would be to dump the nose, pull in the gear and flaps, if they were out, add power, and try to pick up enough speed to fly out of it.

189

Then, when you dumped hydraulic pressure, the spoilers would begin to blow down. But without pressure to regulate their blow-down rate, the fluid in the extension cylinders would bleed back through the orifices unevenly. This would lead to asymmetrical flight spoiler extension and an increasing rolling moment. With the flight power shutoff valve in the off position the roll would be increasingly difficult to counteract because of high control loads in the unboosted situation, so you'd likely panic and put the valve back on. The spoilers would redeploy and you'd add more speed in an effort to regain control.

At some speed, something would finally give. It would probably be the linkage on one ground spoiler, which would blow down, allowing the flight spoilers on that one side to also retract, and the airplane would go into an uncontrollable roll. The NTSB believes that that entire sequence is indeed what happened over Kline, South Carolina.

But now, after having played the "What If" game, the sequence of events can be different. Now if the spoilers ever deploy in flight, you should know what to do about it. First, drop the nose and pick up just enough speed to regain firm pitch and roll control. Never mind that you're descending, the danger is in breaking something with too much speed. Add power slowly and raise the nose cautiously to arrest the descent as much as possible. But keep the speed from getting out of hand. (In fact, with all the boards out a G–II will fly level, and even climb at some weights.)

Next, dump the hydraulic pressure and be ready to ride out the transitory rolling moment as the boards bleed down asymmetrically. You may even roll all the way around, but with elevator control to keep the nose up, a slow roll should present no problem in a G–II. By the time you return to level, the boards should have blown down into the trail position and the danger will be past.

The "What If" game: You should spend a lot of time playing

it. What if a reverser deploys in flight? How would you recognize the problem? What would you do to overcome it? What if the flaps start up asymmetrically? What if you lose all the fuel transfer pumps on one side? What if you lose all rudder control? What if an aileron trim tab motor runs away?

You can see that the "What If" game can be endless. Every pilot should become adept at it, for it's a game you cannot lose.

Passenger Evacuation (October 1977)

In mid–September of 1977 the NTSB issued a recommendation to the FAA that does not reflect well on corporate operators. As a result, it's certain that a lot more attention is going to be directed at the question of passenger evacuation preparedness in business aviation. The recommendations stem from the crash of a Falcon 20 a year ago. Here is the entire text of the Board's letter to FAA Administrator Langhorne Bond.

> On November 12, 1976, a Dassault Falcon fanjet crashed at Naples, Florida. The National Transportation Safety Board's investigation revealed that the nine passengers encountered severe difficulties in evacuating the aircraft because the passengers lacked knowledge of emergency procedures; they were not briefed before departure; and there were no placarded instructions for opening the main cabin door and the two overwing exits.
>
> Specifically, although a passenger briefing is required by 14 CFR 91.199, the pilots did not brief the passengers before takeoff regarding the location and operation of the main door and the overwing exits. Some of the passengers rarely flew on company aircraft and one passenger had never flown on a company aircraft until the day of the accident. None of the passengers could recall having been briefed by a pilot. Al-

though several passenger briefing cards were available in the cabin, the passengers were not directed to refer to them before takeoff.

In addition, the passenger who occupied the jumpseat did not know that a shoulder harness was available for his use even though he had occupied the jumpseat on several occasions. Although this upper torso restraint was only a single diagonal strap, the Safety Board believes that his chest injuries would have been averted had he worn the restraint.

The Safety Board also found that, while a placard was attached to the main entry door containing instructions for closing the door, there were no instructions for opening the main entry door. The passenger in the jumpseat tried to open the door after the accident, but he was not able to do so because he did not know that the three door controls had to be actuated in sequence and that the door had to be pushed outward while simultaneously actuating the controls. The illustration and accompanying written instructions on the passenger briefing cards did not communicate clearly the location, identification and proper sequencing of the door controls. The card also failed to communicate that the door would not open unless the proper sequence was followed.

Requirements for placarding doors are contained in 14 CFR 25.783(b). However, according to the company that installed the interior in the aircraft, the aircraft contained no placards for opening the door when the aircraft was delivered to them. The FAA General Aviation District Office that inspected the aircraft after the interior furnishings were installed did not request that a placard be installed.

The timely evacuation was also affected by the lack of instructions for opening the two overwing exits. Requirements for emergency exit operation placards are contained in 14 CFR 25.811. The passengers correctly actuated the handles which unlocked the two emergency exits, but they did not realize that they also had to grasp the hatches and pull them

inside the cabin. Neither emergency hatch contained placarded instructions to direct the passengers to pull the hatch
away from the fuselage opening. As a result, the two overwing exits were not opened. Our investigation disclosed that
the passenger safety card incorrectly illustrated the overwing
exit hatch configuration installed in that aircraft.

Finally, a small carpet on the floor at the main entrance
area became wedged underneath the door which separates
the passenger cabin from the main entrance area. As a result,
the door jammed closed. Placards on this intra–cabin door
warned that the door was to remain open during takeoff and
landing, but the jumpseat passenger had closed the door before takeoff. The passengers in the cabin were unable to open
the door; thus, access to the main entry door was blocked until
the carpet was removed.

Those findings prompted the Board to issue the following two
recommendations to the FAA:

Issue an Operations Bulletin to alert FAA inspectors of the
need to bring to the attention of Part 91 corporate aircraft
operators the need for:

(a) Briefing of passengers before takeoff on emergency
procedures.

(b) Compliance with placarded instructions on doors which
are required to be open during takeoff and landing.

(c) Stowing of all loose items in the aircraft before takeoff
and landing.

(d) Periodically reviewing the adequacy of passenger
briefing cards.

Issue a Maintenance Bulletin to request FAA inspectors to
review the proper installation and adequacy of placarded instructions for opening all exits on large corporate aircraft.

The next move after such recommendations is inevitable.
Henceforth you can expect to find FAA inspectors crawling all

over your aircraft. They're going to be rewriting all your placards, redesigning your passenger briefing cards—or telling you to get some if you don't now have them—and rehearsing you on the proper method of giving pretakeoff and prelanding passenger briefings.

More important, publication of these recommendations has put a dangerous liability monkey on the back of every business aircraft operator. If we don't tighten up our practices in evacuation preparedness, the liability suits are going to become even more damaging.

To reduce that risk, keep these points in mind:

• You should instantly pull and inspect all the emergency exits in your aircraft. (There may be exceptions to this, as in the case of certain light twins in which pulling the exit involves destructively yanking out the Plexiglas itself.) In some cases that exercise will be a shock, because you'll find the interior has been installed in such a way that either special maneuvering of the exit is required to get it out, or that some interior fixture actually reduces the size of the exit opening.

• Review all emergency exit placards and instructions. This should include tests with people who are unfamiliar with the aircraft. Call out some of the downtown office workers and ask them to remove exits and open the door with no instructions other than those provided by the placards. Document these tests with naive subjects and file the documents with your legal department.

• Brief all your pilots on proper evacuation procedures. You will do well to write an evacuation plan with assumptions involving crewmember incapacitation. Conduct crew drills and document satisfactory performance.

The need for a cabin evacuation is an unpleasant prospect, but that's no excuse for being unprepared.

TECHNIQUES

Thrust Control (October 1973)

Three times each year, on the average, NTSB accident investigations turn up information that indicates pilots are bending airplanes because they don't know it's sometimes necessary to yank power levers closed just when all the instincts of self–preservation are urging that they be pushed farther forward.

Of course, it is easy for us to sit at a typewriter and admonish a turbine pilot on a tight takeoff to pull his power back in event of a compressor stall or a suspected reverser deployment, and to tell the pilot of a light twin to yank the throttles closed and land the airplane in the nearest open space if an engine quits just after liftoff.

It's an altogether different thing, though, to be in the left seat looking out on rows of apartments or a pile of rocks when the compressors stall, a reverser opens, or one engine dies. In that situation, the overwhelming inclination is to maintain a stiff right arm, come what may. For that reason it's especially important for us all to make doubly sure we thoroughly understand *why* the power controls must be pulled back under certain circumstances.

First, let's look back at the compressor–stall situation in a turbine–powered aircraft. Several large and respected turbine training schools, including at least one at an airline and another at a factory, need to have their wrists slapped for neglecting this subject. It's a rare pilot (even among several we've talked with just after they'd completed a factory–approved school), who knows that following FOD (foreign object damage) to a turbine engine, it often will not develop power at all with the power lever full forward, but will run nicely at a partial setting. The reason is due to disrupted air flow at high compressor rpm—commonly referred to as *compressor stall.*

The recommended practice for restoring partial power, spelled out clearly in most engine manufacturers' manuals, is to pull the

195

power control *back*. This clears the stall and the control can then be advanced until enough rpm is regained to drag around the airport and land, which is a nice thing to know in event of FOD to both engines.

So, although every fiber in your body and every one of your animal instincts says to shove the levers forward after FOD, doing so is not likely to get you anything except a face full of bricks. Pilots need to study their engine manuals and then think about this carefully before each departure—particularly those from trashy, wet, or icy runways, or when there is a possibility of birds in the departure path.

What we're advocating is not just for jet pilots. The same thing can happen to the turboprops. When it does, come *back* on the power and attempt to clear the stall. More about that in the following section.

Next, consider the inadvertent thrust reverser deployment incident. Murphy's Law says that what can happen, will happen; thus, on occasion, some crew is going to find itself in a turbine–powered airplane with one engine trying to go and the other trying to whoa.

This is not an easy thing to recognize because as often as not, such a condition is the result of a machine gone berserk. It can happen with absolutely no indication in the cockpit except a hell of a lot of buffeting and a rapidly falling airspeed.

The wise pilot, therefore, maintains an alertness for that possibility and develops an instinct to snatch back the power levers (one at a time, remember) whenever something happens that can't be explained but *could* be a reverser deployed on a jet or a prop reversed in a turboprop.

With the airspeed heading towards V_{SO}, it'll take a lot of moxie to do it, but when nothing else works, you might as well try reducing power on first one engine and then the other. After all, it's better to hit the ground at idle than at full bore.

196

Again, the foregoing should not be read over lightly by turbo-prop pilots and then be forgotten. Props can also reverse inadvertently. A number of years ago there was a notorious airline accident at Newark from that cause. (The airplane was a piston Convair, but the result was the same.) The engines were at partial power when the reversal occurred, but the pilot—thinking he'd had a power failure—did the normal thing and shoved both throttles full up. The aircraft practically did a pirouette into an apartment building.

Finally, let's look again at engine failure in non–FAR 25 piston twins. Probably 95 percent of the time, maybe 99 percent, that second engine is an asset to safety; the rest of the time it's a liability. If an engine quits at any time during the takeoff or early climb, or during an attempted go–around, the chances are good that the airplane will not fly. Moreover, the NTSB statistics show that when a twin crashes with only one engine running, the chance of someone getting killed is *four times* as high as it would have been had the airplane crashed with *no* engine running.

The message is clear. When flying a piston twin close to the ground, *both* throttles should be grasped firmly and the airplane flown as though it had a single engine. That is, if anything happens to one engine, pull both throttles back and land or, at most, use the one good engine to stretch the glide to a more suitable place to crash.

As I admitted in the beginning, all of this is much easier to write about in the comfort of an office than to do in the left seat of an airplane. There is one trick I learned from a senior airline pilot many years ago, however, that might help. Before every flight he always played the "What If" game mentioned earlier. Before cranking up he would sit in the cockpit, alone if possible, and vicariously fly the entire route, asking himself at each stage, "What If that, or this, or this happens?"

If more of us would play the "What If" game and predetermine to pull the power back in event of FOD, an inadvertent reversal, or an engine failure at low speeds in a piston twin, many lives would be saved.

Clear the Stall (September 1973)

Few corporate aviation accidents in recent times have attracted as much attention as the crash of the Machinery Buyers Corporation Learjet 24 after ingesting birds on departure from DeKalb–Peachtree Airport in Atlanta in February of 1973—nor has any recent corporate aviation tragedy resulted in as much improvement in aviation safety.

The accident attracted such attention because it caused a totally senseless and unnecessary loss of seven lives. The birds were attracted to the departure path of the Learjet by a garbage dump operated by DeKalb County, which also operates the airport. The county repeatedly was warned by the FAA, beginning in 1970, that the dump constituted a hazard. In February 1971, two years before the accident, the county finally gave in and told the FAA the dump would be closed within 18 months. However, the promise wasn't kept. Two years after the promise, the birds killed these seven people.

After the accident, the FAA went to court and forced the county to act. DeKalb–Peachtree is now a much safer airport, and because of the notoriety of the accident and pressure from the aviation press, airport operators everywhere have become more aware of the bird problem and have acted to alleviate it. Consequently, we're all a little safer at a great many airports around the country.

There was yet another benefit from the accident, however, which has often been overlooked. Even the NTSB skipped over it lightly in its report. The fact is noted, but the report does not follow through with the practical application. To explain, let's look at the accident.

The aircraft, N454RN, departed DeKalb–Peachtree at 1012 local time on an IFR flight plan to Miami. The weather was ceiling 500 feet, visibility four miles. Although the wind was 060 at four knots, the Learjet departed on 20 Left. After watching it make a normal takeoff, tower personnel noted a trail of blue–white or blue–gray smoke from the left engine as the aircraft crossed the airport boundary. The crew was notified and one of them replied, "We just hit some birds." The tower asked if they would turn to land. The reply was, simply, "Don't believe we're gonna make it."

The crew displayed extraordinary calm. The aircraft was maneuvered to avoid crashing directly into an apartment complex, and apparently there was an unsuccessful attempt to relight the left engine. In spite of these efforts, the Learjet glanced off a roof and crashed into a wooded ravine.

Minutes after the crash, 15 dead cowbirds were found within 150 feet of the departure end of Runway 20L. Bird residue and feathers were found on the aircraft windshield and centerpost, and both engines showed distortion and foreign–object damage to the compressor rotor assemblies. The NTSB said that blade damage indicated 14 bird strikes against the left engine, while the right engine had at least five.

In the course of the investigation, the NTSB referred back to the original certification tests of the General Electric CJ610 engines. "During these tests," the NTSB said, "chloroformed birds similar to starlings weighing two to four ounces were fired consecutively into the engine at speeds from 69 to 175 knots. With the throttle held at the *takeoff position*, the engine stalled after ingesting of a single bird . . . but at least 87 percent speed and 66 percent power was obtained after *retarding the throttle to idle and slowly advancing it until stall was again encountered.*"

The emphasis is mine. The NTSB neither emphasized it in the report, nor followed up with the observation that this is a valuable —in fact crucial—technique for restoring at least partial power to a turbine engine after FOD.

Yet one doesn't have to look far to find turbine–rated pilots who have never heard of the procedure. Of the first five pilots I talked to about the Atlanta accident, three were unaware of the technique, although one had just completed a factory transition school on a business jet.

Interestingly, engineers are quite familiar with it. One I've talked with had a manual at his elbow that explained the procedure in depth. The GE CJ610/CF700 information manual is precise and clear. Although it probably wouldn't have helped the crew of N454RN—the damage to those engines was too severe—this knowledge is something every pilot should be prepared to use on each takeoff or landing. For that reason, let's look at the pertinent sections of the GE manual:

> CJ610/CF700 Jet Engine Flight Operations and Performance Notes: Although these engines are considered stall–free engines, a malfunction of the control system, foreign–object damage to the compressor, an extreme attitude flight maneuver or an extremely "dirty" compressor can cause a stall. For that reason a pilot should know how to recognize and deal with a stall should one occur.
>
> Compressor stalls may be recognized by a sudden rise in EGT, rpm hangup or drop and a rapid audible change in characteristic sound of normal engine operation (an explosive sound if stall is severe enough). Successful recovery from a stall depends on how far the condition has progressed and a continued stalled condition will result in engine flameout and excessive damage to the engine. Early recognition will increase the possibility of a successful recovery and lessen the chance of damage from overtemperature. When a stall is

recognized, it can be cleared by immediately retarding the throttle to idle (minimum flight idle if applicable), allowing the stall to clear itself, then slowly (six–eight seconds) advancing the throttle to the desired setting. When stable engine condition is regained, check all engine parameters (i.e., rpm, EGT, F/F and EPR), to determine if normal operation can be continued. If normal operation can be regained, continue normal operation and perform a thorough inspection for engine damage as soon as possible. However, if normal operation cannot be regained because the stall reoccurs, operate the engine below the stall rpm or perform shutdown (according to pilot's discretion) and perform required maintenance as soon as possible.

The reason the procedure works is straightforward. When a foreign object is ingested, the normal result is distortion of the compressor blades, guide vanes, or inlet—sometimes all three. To over–simplify, this distorts the internal airflow patterns, which leads to compressor stall. The higher the rpm, the greater the airflow disruption by a bent blade, and as long as the rpm remains high the stall continues.

To "clear the stall," rpm must be reduced until the airflow pattern is within tolerance. The rpm can then be increased just to the onset of airflow disruption. Tests have shown that as much as 50 percent of an engine's power (about 85 percent rpm) can be restored by this technique after it has ingested as many as four birds—or, of course, sustained an equivalent amount of damage due to slush or ice ingestion. Many jets, coincidentally, will maintain level flight on 50 percent power from a single engine at normal operating weights.

It is imperative that every turbine aircraft pilot familiarize himself with the procedures for clearing a compressor stall in his engines. You may have to go directly to the engine manufacturer, because the information is seldom found in flight manuals.

It goes against all instincts, but being prepared to pull the throttles back (one at a time, naturally), and advancing them slowly can make the difference whenever the popping or chugging of a compressor stall is heard immediately after a takeoff on slush or through birds.

If having that knowledge should ever save your life, a salute to Ernie Selfors and Dave Phillips (pilot and copilot of the Machinery Buyers' Learjet) would be in order.

The Out-of-Gas Accident (January 1974)

In a 1972 NTSB computer study of accidents involving engine failure, the Board found that 18.8 percent of them were the result of simply running the tanks dry.

Though flying an airplane out of fuel is an obvious thing not to do, history shows that not doing so is something that must be learned. It seems that until a pilot has crossed the runway threshold a few times with the gauges on empty and the taste of fear in his mouth, the possibility, and possible consequences, of running flat out of fuel doesn't make much of an impression.

I must confess that in my youth I landed several times and then watched the lineman put a gallon or two *more* fuel in the tanks than the usable capacity. After that sort of thing happens a few times, the message finally gets across.

The NTSB lists causes for fuel exhaustion accidents in the following sequence: inadequate preflight preparation, mismanagement of fuel, improper inflight decisions, becoming lost, inattention to fuel supply, miscalculated consumption. We can assume that you readers do not get lost or mismanage the tank selection process or forget to look at the gauges every now and then. So let's look at those other three causes to see what can be done to cut down on the frequency.

TECHNIQUES

Inadequate preparation

——Probably 90 percent of the problem can be solved here. You've heard this before, but preparation *is* professionalism. These are the important points:

• The first thing that must be done in fuel planning a flight is to decide whether a stop will be necessary. In view of the uncertainty of being able to get the proper grade of fuel at all airports these days, you must decide on two things. First, do you have the range to go nonstop—with safe reserves? Just because you *can* go nonstop no longer means you should, however, because the second question is: Can you get fuel at your destination? The trick nowadays is never to get caught on the ground without adequate fuel to go somewhere else if necessary. That can be achieved by either refueling en route or calling ahead to make an ironclad deal for fuel at your destination.

• If you must refuel en route, try to stop at the mid point. If you must refuel twice, break the trip into three equal legs. It seems that every time I break this rule I get into trouble. On a flight from Washington to Fort Lauderdale some years ago, the rule called for refueling at Savannah. But coming up on Savannah the gauges were still way up and it seemed a waste to drop down, top off, then climb up again, so I decided to continue to Jacksonville and refuel there. I arrived at Jacksonville neck and neck with a thunderstorm, but I'd used up options at Savannah, and so had to shoot an approach into the teeth of the storm with near empty tanks.

Regardless of thunderstorms and the possibility of arriving overhead and discovering someone gear–up in the middle of the only runway, we must now be aware of possible fuel outages at some airports. Again, then, to avoid the obvious temptation, don't let yourself get caught on the ground without adequate fuel to go elsewhere in a pinch. Break the trip into equal stages rather than a long one and a short one.

• Check the level of your tanks carefully before departure. With fuel prices what they are these days, theft may become more prevalent. It's easy for anyone who knows about airplanes to drain off five or 10 gallons for their car. Add to that the possibility that a thief won't know how to replace caps correctly and it becomes especially important for you to look in each tank personally before departure.

Improper inflight decisions

——If your preplanning was adequate, an inflight fuel decision should not be necessary. However, even with the best of planning, headwinds are sometimes greater than forecast, the destination weather goes to pot, or a mechanical can leave you with fuel onboard you cannot use. The instant you discover that the winds are stronger than forecast, get on Unicom and begin asking who nearby has some fuel. Do the same thing if the weather goes down at your prearranged refueling stop, or when a fuel pump fails that could prevent transfer from a critical tank.

Miscalculated consumption

——Assuming you keep records of consumption on every trip and watch the time, this shouldn't happen.

Even doing that, however, a pilot can still run into a problem after a departure with partial tanks. One of the things we can do to get more miles per pound of fuel is to haul only the pounds needed for the trip. This practice must, of course, be balanced against the safety measures enumerated above—and it presupposes a method of determining precisely how much fuel is in a partially filled tank.

204

In the final analysis, the chief and only certain way to deal with fuel exhaustion is discipline. Every pilot should pick a low–fuel condition beyond which he will not remain aloft under any circumstances.

One in 20 fuel exhaustion accidents results in someone getting killed. Those are poor odds for an accident type as dumb as running out of fuel.

The Basics of IFR (December 1975)

In December 1974, a Northwest Airlines 727 crashed about 11 minutes after departing JFK in New York on a ferry flight to Buffalo. There was weather and heavy turbulence in the area at the time of the accident, and a crewmember on the aircraft broadcast a Mayday 10 minutes after departure saying the crew had lost control of the plane, which was descending through FL200, then 12,000 feet, in a stall. The NTSB investigators found that the probable cause was loss of control resulting from iced–over pitot heads and static ports.

The conjecture—supported by very good evidence—is that the pitot heads iced over at about 16,000 feet. As a result, the continued climb caused a false increase in the indicated airspeeds. As the IAS increased the crew raised the nose to counteract it. That led to an even greater climb rate and consequently an accelerated rise in the false IAS. This condition caused the crew to pull back on the elevator even harder. Finally, the airplane stalled and spun.

Other pilots flying in the area at the time reported picking up ice at about 16,000 feet and an exhaustive investigation by the NTSB led to a conclusion that the pitot heats were not turned on prior to departure, as called for in the checklist.

When a pitot head and/or its associated static source ices over, the ambient pressure is trapped in the lines leading to one or both sides of the instruments. This will cause an interesting thing to occur to airspeed readings. Let's let the NTSB describe it:

> In event of a blocked pitot or static system, the direction of the indicated airspeed error would depend on which of the systems was blocked and the direction of change in the ambient static pressure. Under conditions where the pressure in the static system increases with respect to the pressure in the pitot system, the indicated airspeed will read low erroneously. For the opposite condition, where the pressure in the static system decreases with respect to the pressure in the pitot system, the indicated airspeed will read high erroneously. The latter would exist if the pitot head was blocked so that a constant pressure was trapped in the pitot system while the aircraft was ascending. This is because the static system pressure would decrease and the resultant differential pressure would appear as an increase in airspeed.
>
> Indicated airspeed error may also occur when the pitot system becomes insensitive to changes in total pressure in such a manner that the system vents to an ambient static pressure source. The pressure measured by the pitot system will equalize with the pressure in the static system, and the dynamic pressure (indicated airspeed) will decrease to zero. The vent source in a pitot head which can produce this kind of error is the moisture drain hole, which is located downstream from a blocked total pressure sensing inlet.

This condition is something that must be thoroughly understood by every pilot. When a pitot head or static vent is blocked, the indicated airspeed does not necessarily drop to zero. In continued level flight, it may not do anything; it may continue to display the IAS that prevailed when the blockage occurred, and so you may not even notice the problem until there is an altitude change. If you know this, there is no excuse for a blockage to cause you any more than an inconvenience; if you don't, the results can be horrifying. Again quoting from the NTSB report:

> The airspeed and the altitude values which were recorded (on the flight data recorder) were consistent with the airspeed's predicted climb performance until the aircraft reached 16,000 feet (the altitude at which the pitot evidently froze over). The simultaneous increases in both airspeed and rate of ascent which were recorded thereafter exceeded the theoretical performance capability of a B–727–200 series aircraft of the same weight as N274US. Consequently, the recorded (hence, displayed) airspeed values were suspected to be erroneous, and it appeared that they varied directly with the change in recorded altitude. The recorded airspeeds correlated within five percent with the theoretical airspeeds which would be expected if the pressure measured in the pitot system has remained constant after the aircraft's climb through 16,000 feet.

> The . . . airspeed of the aircraft when the stick shaker was first activated was calculated to be 165 knots as compared to the 412 knots recorded by the FDR. The decrease in airspeed from 305 knots to 165 knots as the aircraft climbed from 16,000 feet to 24,000 feet (within 16 seconds) is within the aircraft's theoretical climb power performance. The aircraft's pitch attitude would have been about 30 degrees nose–up as stick–shaker speed was approached. The stall–warning stick shaker is activated by angle–of–attack instrumentation which is completely independent of, and therefore not affected by errors in, the aircraft's airspeed measuring systems.

> Vertical acceleration reduced slightly as the aircraft leveled at 24,800 feet probably because the pilot relaxed the back pressure being applied to the control column. The stick shaker ceased momentarily; however, the aircraft continued to decelerate because of the drag induced by the high body attitude, and the stick shaker reactivated. Boeing personnel interpre-

ted the sound of the landing gear warning horn on the CVR to indicate that the thrust levers had been retarded to idle. The second reduction in vertical acceleration—to 0.8 G which was coincident with a sudden descent and a rapid magnetic heading change—was probably caused by an aerodynamic stall with a probable loss of lateral control.

Theoretical relationships of angle of attack, velocity and drag were compared to the recorded rate of descent and load factor to determine the attitude of the aircraft after the stall. The comparison showed that the aircraft attained an angle of attack of 22 degrees, or greater, during the descent. Transient nose–down attitudes of more than 60 degrees would have been required to achieve the measured descent rate with an angle of attack of 22 degrees. The variations in load factors, which averaged about +1.5 G, were attributed to variations in the aircraft's angle of bank.

The aircraft was probably exceeding 230 knots, with a nose–down attitude of about 50 degrees as it descended below 11,000 feet, when the flaps were extended to two degrees. The momentary cessation of the stick shaker indicated that the angle of attack had been reduced to less than 13 degrees. The increase in vertical acceleration to 2.5 G was attributed to the aircraft's being in a tight nose–down spiral with a bank angle between 70 degrees and 80 degrees.

Can you imagine what it was like on that flight deck when the IAS hit 412 knots and the overspeed warning horn and stick shaker went off simultaneously?

More important, can you understand why the crew didn't recognize a 30–degree nose–up attitude? When the stall warner went off, everyone on the flight deck assumed it was Mach buffet. The first officer commented, "There's that Mach buffet, guess we'll have to pull it up." This was followed by the captain's command, "Pull it up."

The flight deck conversations do not indicate that any crewmember ever noted the nose–up attitude on the artificial horizon. The crew evidently thought they were in some sort of tremendous updraft and were actually climbing 6000 fpm at an IAS of 412 knots. The lessons for us are extremely clear.

First, always get those pitot heats on whenever there is the slightest chance of ice. It's a good idea to turn them on any time you're in visible moisture regardless of the OAT.

Second, *fly attitude.*

The crucial lesson from this accident is one that should be pounded into every student pilot from the day he first walks onto the airport: FLY ATTITUDE. Any time controllability begins to be a problem—and even when you just plain don't understand what's going on—leveling the airplane off, either visually or by instruments, will start to get you out of trouble. This must be done with careful attention to G forces, of course, but once the airplane is level, and kept level, there's not much in nature that can hurt it.

It's possible that the gyros had tumbled in this 727 (though there's absolutely nothing to indicate they did), but even then a properly trained pilot should have been able to maintain a reasonably safe attitude. All he needs to do is set up a power and trim situation that previous investigations have shown will result in level flight, then concentrate on stopping the turns.

If you haven't worked this out in the airplane you fly, you'd better do it right away. Cover the airspeed, VSI, AH, DG and altimeter on a VFR day and work out a procedure that will keep the airplane right side up and within speed limits regardless of turbulence.

Granted, there are some high–performance airplanes that simply cannot be flown without some kind of attitude reference. But there's always something on the modern jet panel that'll give the pilot enough of a reference to allow a reasonable attitude to be maintained.

Of course, you should always remember to scan *all* the instru-

209

ments—especially when control of the aircraft is in doubt. In turbulent air, attitude is primary. Look at it often.

You must also be prepared to recognize the difference between an impending stall and Mach buffet. There are a number of system anomalies and flight situations that can leave you guessing. Recognition will come from having experienced and thought about each beforehand in a controlled situation.

To recap: At the first indication of unnatural speed and climb indications, someone in this 727 should have turned on the pitot heats. Even failing that, had this crew not been mesmerized by the *indicated* airspeed and rate of climb, the accident could have been avoided by simply going to the attitude gyros and flying a normal pitch schedule. If the gyros *were* tumbled, a *previously investigated* power and trim condition could have been used to maintain control until someone remembered to turn on the pitot heats.

This is another case of someone not playing the old "What If" game. If you haven't asked yourself "What If the airspeed fails" followed by "What If both airspeed and gyros fail," you're setting on a mighty short fuse.